The Good One
RISES
(La Taína Sube)

Mynet Velez

HONOR FIRST
PRESS

The Good One Rises
La Taína Sube
© 2021 by Mynet Velez
Illustrations by Mynet Velez

Printed in the United States of America.
ISBN-13: 978-1-7372768-7-6
LCCN: xxxx

HONOR FIRST PRESS
Daytona Beach, Florida

HONOR FIRST
PRESS

With the greatest love from my heart, I dedicate this book to my sons, Michael R. Mills-Vélez and Manuel R. Mills-Vélez. You are my legacy, the reason I breathe and bring balance within my universe.

Thank you to my father, the Honorable Amilkar Vélez-López, my mother, Ada Myrna Quiñones and my step-mother, Norma Iris Mutt-Vélez for raising me to know who I am, and never letting me forget it. To my brother, Amilkar (Miko) Vélez and my sister, Katilia Y. Vélez, you embody all the passion and warrior spirit our ancestors possessed.

To my brother through love, Keith Kelly and my cousins, Luz (Chiqui) Rios, Kristina Ibañez, & my best friend/sister through love M. Lashway: thank you for giving me the courage to write what has been shared in my dreams. Thank you, my soul-sister Janet M. Solorzano, and my prima through love Cadesha Johnson for always standing beside me for more than 3 decades.

And to my love of my life, Roy Benjamin Durón, may the universe continue to guide us in our long life together always beside each other.

May Atabey always protect us, the Great Spirit continue to guide us, and may we always embody honor first in everything we do.

Love,
Mynet

Foreword by the Author

To understand the story of Atabeira and the people whom we refer to today as the Taíno, I will share with you a brief history of the colonization of what is now known as the Caribbean, and what happened to the indigenous people of what is now known as Puerto Rico. This is a brief de-colonized version of the history of our islands and our ancestors. You will see similarities all around the world if you choose to learn what is not in traditional textbooks, inclusive of the Atlantic slave trades.

In 1492, Christopher Columbus, financed by King Ferdinand and Queen Isabella of Spain, reached the island of Ayití/Quisqueya, now known as Haiti and the Dominican Republic. At the time, Columbus renamed it Insula España/La Isla Española and subsequently was renamed again, Española. The island areas were inhabited by indigenous people the Spaniards named Taíno: a word in their native language meaning "Good One." Erroneously believing that the lighter skinned people arriving from the vessels were a part of an ancient myth of deities sent to them for salvation, the indigenous people (for the most part) were not initially resistant to the occupation of their land. The sailors arriving from Spain, Portugal, and later from France were not there for a collaborative relationship other than to use the people of the island(s) for mining and stripping the land of its resources. Supported by the Roman

Catholic Church, the people of the island(s) were enslaved and used for their selfish ends, inclusive of converting the indigenous people to Christianity, genocide of the indigenous peoples who were deemed 'savages' and, stripping them of their culture, religion, and sentient identity.

Having written to the King Ferdinand and Queen Isabella of Spain about the geniality of the people, and presenting them with riches taken from the island, Columbus set sail again in 1493 towards Española. However, he miscalculated and arrived on the island of Boriken, renamed it San Juan Bautista and repeated the same invasion of the island and its people.

Each character in the trilogy has their own voice, their own perspective, and their own experience. I hope you will come away knowing some more about the history of our islands, and that our indigenous people are not dead. They are not gone, and indeed are still living in the faces of every person whose lineage can be traced back to the islands... regardless of what they may look like. Our indigenous language has also survived time and occupation, with many words of things and events adopted by many cultures such as jamaca (hammock), juracan (hurricane) and canoa (canoe), to name a few. I have included indigenous words with their translations within the chapters so you can have a greater authenticity in your understanding of the real history of the island of Boriken; and how it was replicated with impunity in the Americas and around the world. The spelling may not be perfect as there was no written language, but it is close based on research and what we now know of the indigenous people of the islands.

May the great spirit always be with you. Taíno-tí au tauguey.

~Mynet

"They traded with us and gave us everything they had, with good will...they took great delight in pleasing us...They are very gentle and without knowledge of what is evil; nor do they murder or steal...Your highness may believe that in all the world there can be no better people...They love their neighbors as themselves, and they have the sweetest talk in the world, and are gentle and always laughing."

~ Christopher Columbus, Letter to King Ferdinand of Spain, 1492

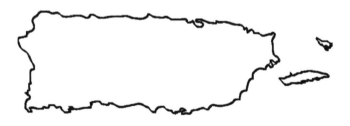

The Good One Rises

(La Taína Sube)

<u>1510</u>

Atabeira perched herself on the mid-level branch in the middle of the rainforest's tree. Her dark eyes glared into the dusk scanning for any and all movement on the ground. She adjusted her bare feet on the branch to maintain her balance while her nagua[1] flowed with her movement. Her dagger strapped to her leg in its sheath, in case she needed it. Softening her breathing, she listened for harsh steps that the ghosts, the Spaniards who invaded her Borikén[2] years ago, were known to make as they trampled over the sacred forests

---

[1]   Nagua: a cottonlike cloth that people used in the Taíno culture. It was a straight cloth tied at the waist by a rope.

[2]   Borikén: the original name of Borinquen in the Taíno Taino language before the Spaniards invaded. It is the area now known as Puerto Rico.

heading north with the clunky botas[3] on their nasty feet. *They are so dumb,* she thought to herself. Slowly exhaling, she gripped her macana[4] with ease as she anticipated her attack.

As the glow of the falling sunlight glistened on her coppery skin, her eyes picked up her brethren in their places all throughout the trail. She could feel the tension in the air growing... waiting on the arrival of the evil ones who tricked their people, and poisoned their world with lies, violence and treachery. Some of them already had their weapons at the ready; their steely eyes narrowed under their flat brow with their legs ready to spring. Some of the others had their macanas and the Spanish daggers they took off the ones they defeated in past battles in their hands, while one held the new machete in their grip. Red and black body paint helped to conceal them among the branches. Then, she heard the sound! *CRUNCH! CRUNCH!* Followed by the unmistakable whistle from her brother warrior to the south,

"Ko-Ki! Ko-Ko-Ko-Ki!"

Atabeira's heartbeat roared in her ears. Her breath deepened with every crunch she heard. The now familiar Castilian words in chatter coming from the invaders who were oblivious to the pack above their very heads. She was in the middle of the pack among the trees. The first series of whistles was to warn they entered the area. They were told it was to be a small contingent moving to the north side of the mountains to fetch for the don his new play-toy, the daughter of a collaborator

---

[3] Botas: Spanish word for "boots," usually made of leather, wood and some metal.

[4] Macana: a wooden club, fashioned like a sword or machete with sharpened edges.

cacique who avoided trouble at all costs. *Not today evil ones... not today.* She waited for the signal from the north side of the trail.

"Ko-Ko-Ko-Ki! Ko-Ki!"

Yes! She grinned to herself.

"Ja!"[5] She roared at the top of her lungs. Leaping from the branch as she swung her macana to the soldier's open face; the entire contingent looked up in horror to see the fury of copper, red and black raining from above.

---

[5] Ja: pronounced "Ha!"

Part 1: heketi

1504

"Oooff!" Atabeira exhaled loudly as the batu[6] missed her stone belt and landed squarely on her stomach. *I can't believe I missed that,* she thought to herself.

Her cousin, Yukogueybana doubled over in laughter.

"Hope that didn't hurt too much," he teased as he ran past her towards the ball, patting her on the shoulder along the way.

He already passed her in height years ago and Yuko loved to tease her as a big brother would. His straight black hair stuck to the sweat off his flat brow as he grinned looking back at her.

"Try to pass this one off better," he shouted as he kicked the batu towards her again.

Atabeira hated being the smallest one of the group, but she loved playing batey[7] with them. Even the brothers from the neighboring village weren't as big as Yuko but they were

---

[6] Batu: a rubber ball commonly used in the game of Batey. A ceremonial stone belt called a Yuke, the legs, thighs or shoulders could be used to hit the ball into the opposing team. Men and women played together. It is reminiscent of the modern-day soccer.

[7] Batey: a game similar to modern day soccer played in teams of 12 versus 12.

getting faster and more muscular with each passing moon phase. Rituraybanamu was older by 2 years and growing thoughtful in his expressions, but still loved being called by his nickname Turay. Gueriobanamu was loud and brash, flashing his dimples when he smiled brightly like the sun. Hence, the reason he was always referred to as Guey.[8] You would never find the brothers far apart from each other. Where one was, the other was surely nearby.

She tapped the ball with her shoulder and deftly swung it towards the goal. All she had to do was to angle it to the stone on the side and then…

"Bei! Here! I'm open!" she turned to the voice and saw her best friend Hutiacaona yelling to her and waving her arms in an open spot just opposite to where Atabeira was looking. Sure enough, she was open with no one defending against her.

The row of rounded stones was behind Hutia's lithe frame keeping the young ones outside of the game as they cheered for the players. Atabeira was quick to redirect the ball to Hutia, who only had to sidestep a little bit to gain control and score.

"Ja!" Everyone on her team celebrated together.

Atabeira felt strong muscular arms wrap around her neck from behind. As she reached up to grab the forearms, she heard a familiar brash voice whisper loudly.

"Nice save. How are you going to get out of this one though?"

She quickly grabbed the muscular forearm, jumped into a squat and flipped the young man over her hip without trouble.

---

[8] Guey: Taíno word for Sun

Laughing, as she offered her hand to help him up, he winced slightly.

"Aw that didn't hurt much, did it Jaibacovix?" She asked as she laughed.

"I really have to remember, not to attack you from behind," Jaibacovix's eyes crinkled from smiling as he took her hand to stand up.

His bronzed skin was peppered with the dirt that cushioned his fall as he fell to the ground. Shaking his long black hair, he was able to get most of it out. Atabeira brushed his bangs from his flat brow.[9]

"Don't worry, I don't think I embarrassed you... much," she grinned.

"Nyah," he responded sticking his tongue out at her.

Scrunching her face, she stuck her tongue back at him in response.

"Maybe one day you will be as great a fighter as I am."

He looked at her in mock surprise,

"Who? Me?" Jaiba responded laughing amicably.

"Atabeira! Guárico guakía!"[10] Startled, Atabeira heard the sharp voice of her mother from across the village. She hurriedly removed the stone belt from her waist and tossed it to Hutia.

---

[9] A flat brow was a sign of elevated social status. Mothers would tie a stone to their baby's head to flatten the forehead as the baby grew.

[10] Guárico guakía: a Taíno phrase meaning "Come to us"

"Can you please take care of this? Bibi[11] is calling for me and I have to go."

"Of course, go." Hutia replied while catching the belt with ease and turning towards the group of friends to chat before going back to practicing their lessons.

Atabeira jogged towards her mother's bohio[12] on the dirt pathway. The tree line of the forest trimmed the village and the farmlands in luscious shades of green leaves and vines. Her people were very adept at farming and knew how to use the land gifted by the great spirits, Yayael and Atabey. Nothing was taken for granted and all was appreciated. As she jogged towards her mother's home, she passed by her father's great longhouse and peeked to see if he was there to greet him. When she saw her father wasn't there, she sprinted to her mother's house. Bibi's home was just past her Baba's,[13] and if he wasn't there with his other wife, then he was with her mother.

Her father, Oromico, was the cacique[14] of the village. It was custom that a person of his status would have more than one wife. He was a kind and just leader who wanted to keep his people safe, happy and at peace. He was a strong figure even though he was of average height for them. Oromico enjoyed helping others and still participated when he had the opportunity to hunt and farm, imparting his wisdom to the

---

[11] Bibi: Taíno word for "Mother."

[12] Bohio is a traditional Taíno roundhouse made of log and palm leaves.

[13] Baba: Taíno word for "Father"

[14] Cacique: Taíno word for "chief, or leader." The term Cacique used in place of king/queen was interpreted as a way for the invaders to understand hierarchy using the European social structure.

young people of the village. Everyone in the village loved him for his kindness and fondness for festivities. As the cacique, he wore his golden emblem on his chest with pride and a nagua that was embellished with black and red thread and seashells.

Her mother was a petite but strong woman, much like Atabeira. She was a wise woman who was also a healer. Her father loved her very much, but Ari-Anani was not fond of his other wife. Instead of living in friction, she chose to live on her own with Atabeira in her own humble bohio. This was not common, but Oromico did not want to have a home in conflict; so, he agreed. The closer Atabeira got to her Bibi's bohio the stronger the smells of the herbs and medicines that Ari-Anani made grew. She could make out her mother's muscled frame in the doorway; her inagua[15] flowing as she shielded her eyes from the bright sun looking for her daughter. The ropes adorned with shells were twinned thoughtfully around her wrists and ankles. Her black hair had a few streaks of silver accenting her temples, framing her heart shaped face. The kindness in her eyes shone with the wisdom of all the mothers before her as she spotted Atabeira bounding towards their home. She held out her bronzed arms, greeting to her only child.

"Nanichi,"[16] Ari-Anani said softly into her daughter's hair as they embraced. "Hurry. Go greet your father. He is inside and needs to speak to us both."

Atabeira smoothed her black hair as her mother gently wiped some dirt from her round face.

"Ay, you were playing again weren't you?" she admonished.

---

[15] Inagua: similar to a nagua but longer in length, tied to the waist with a rope. Usually used by married women.

[16] Nanichi: Taíno phrase meaning, "My heart" or "My love"

"Only one round." Atabeira responded trying to not sound excited, "we won though! And..."

"Tsst," her mother clicked her tongue to shush her, "Tell me later. Now is the time to greet your Baba."

Atabeira took a deep breath and composed herself. Her mother draped Atabeira's glossy hair down to the front, but revealed the golden earrings decorating her ears. Atabeira was no longer a little girl, but she wasn't yet a woman, so she was not permitted to wear the nagua. Ari-Anani adjusted the bracelet cords with the woven gold and shells around her daughter's wrists so they lay without looking askew and ushered her into the bohio.

Her father was inside near the jamaca[17] on the ture[18] sitting patiently waiting for his favorite daughter to arrive. Joy filled his face when he saw Atabeira rush to greet him.

"Baba!" she exclaimed as she hugged him unceremoniously.

"How's my favorite guazabara?"[19] He asked with laughter in his voice.

He knew she did not care for cooking or farming. All she ever wanted to do was hunt and train to fight. It seemed as if she was obsessed with it, much to his other wife's chagrin. He didn't care though, and indulged Atabeira. Oromico knew she had more skills than most of the young men and women in the village. Besides, he had plenty of daughters to farm and tend to the home in his old age. This one though, she was

---

[17] Jamaca: a hanging bed made of cloth tied up with rope.

[18] Ture: Taíno word for a chair with short legs. Almost like a modern stool.

[19] Guazabara: Taíno word for "warrior", also used interchangeably as "war"

feisty, and he did not want to ever see that light stop shining from her.

"I have brought a gift for you," he said with a twinkle in his eye.

Atabeira glanced all around quickly until she came upon her sleeping mat on the floor and saw it.

"Ja!" She exclaimed in glee running towards the mat.

On top of the sleeping mat was her very own macana! Made of the finest wood, carved and cured to withstand the strongest strikes, it was beautiful and golden like the rays of the sun. She gently picked it up with reverence noticing the details on it.

"Baba! Atabey is with me!" she gasped letting her fingertips run over the etching of the great goddess Atabey whom she was named after.

It wasn't as long as the one that Jaibacovix received from his father, but it was perfect for her size and frame. She held it lovingly.

"Thank you so much!"

"You've earned it nanichi. I fear we may have some challenges coming soon and you must be ready," her Baba answered.

Oromico's lined face flickered with concern for a moment.

"This means that you must train very hard and not miss any of your lessons. Even the farming and home chores." His voice brightened a bit as he spoke to his favorite daughter.

Ari-Anani's petite hands rested softly on his broad shoulders.

"Go show your friends, I know you left them at the batey," her Baba encouraged as he swatted at her lovingly to shoo her out of the bohio.

Atabeira glanced at her mother for approval and her mother nodded with a smile. Atabeira sprinted to the doorway, stopped suddenly, turned and ran into her father's arms. Never seeing the tremor in his lips as he grimaced to control his emotions.

"Thank you, Baba." She pressed her forehead to his and sprinted out of the home.

As Atabeira left, Ari-Anani stepped in front of her husband. Cupping his wide face into the palms of her hands, she looked into his eyes.

"You've seen what I've seen, haven't you?"

She had shared with no one the visions that the spirits shared with her, showing what was to come. Terrifying dreams of darkness and despair. Oromico nodded solemnly.

"I met with them the other day - the white ghosts who came from the large canoas[20] a while ago. Agüeybaná had me meet some of them. He is arranging marriages to solidify an alliance."

"Wúa!"[21] Ari-Anani exclaimed in horror.

Her face overcome with fear, she looked in the direction of the doorway where her daughter had just stood.

---

[20] Canoa: Taíno word for "boat." Typically, they are smaller boats fitting 20 – 100 people. Oromico is referencing the large Spanish ships that were used by the Spanish to anchor just off the island.

[21] Wúa: Taíno word for "No"

"She is too young! She cannot. No... To one of those nasty Spaniards? Do you know what they are doing? What they have done to the women they 'marry'?" Ari-Anani pleaded.

Her eyes darted back and forth as the desperate feeling overwhelmed her. Her visions! *No! Not Atabeira!* Oromico stood and placed his hands on his wife's shoulders from behind her and enveloped her in his strong arms. His voice softened realizing that she was becoming upset and understood what that meeting meant. Holding her, he tried to comfort her and reason with her.

"Shhhhh. I explained that Atabeira is still a child and not of age to marry. But when she is old enough, Agüeybaná may arrange it for us. He assured me that it would be with one of the good ones."

"Good ones? Have you not seen them? They don't even bathe regularly! They are disrespectful and more and more of our people are disappearing daily..." she turned and looked desperately into his eyes. "Can't you see that they are buticaco!"[22]

"We have time," he replied softly, "we must teach all of our young ones, and prepare them for what will come. I keep hoping it will be well for us. Maybe a marriage between our people will be the bridge to have them understand our ways. They asked for men to help mining and I've agreed to keep the peace."

As she looked at him in horror, she replied.

"You know I have seen what is to come..." she desperately wanted him to understand.

---

[22] Buticaco: a Taíno insult meaning "shifty eyes"

15

"It is what it is," he said sharply.

His face grimaced believing that he could do nothing to stop it. She stopped speaking; searching in his eyes for the man she loved. Instead, she realized he was not what she thought he was.

"I will teach her well." As she spoke, her eyes dimmed with the realization of what was to come was already on its way.

He went to touch her hand, but she pulled it sharply away and spoke sternly.

"I hear your other wife calling for you. Best that you go to her now."

He stopped and looked at her quizzically for a moment. Nodding his head, sadness flashed through his eyes as he turned away. As he turned and walked out of her home, Ari-Anani cried from the depths of her soul with the fear of what was to come. "Guákia Bibi[23] Atabey, guide us and protect us." She prayed fervently through her sobs of fear.

1508

Steady... steady. The bow was being pulled tight. The tip of

---

[23] Guákia Bibi: Taíno phrase, "Our Mother"

the arrow tracking the boar, unaware that sights were set on it. From where she was sitting crouched among the brush by the curve of the trail, no one would have been able to see her. Hutiacaona held her breath and released her right hand from the arrow and the taught string. The boar let out a squeal of pain and stumbled. While the arrow didn't kill the boar, it injured it enough to make it flop as it tried to stumble backwards to safety. As it flopped miserably, Atabeira leaped from a low branch of the tree where the boar was headed, and her macana landed perfectly on his neck, killing him instantly.

"Yes! Nice!" Turay exclaimed as he half-jogged with Hutia to where she was standing over the boar.

"I was aiming right at it. I don't know what happened." Hutia gestured to the middle of its body.

The arrow had pierced the front leg and pinned it to the body which was why it flopped instead of running away. Her oval face, which usually held a ready smile, frowned in consternation. Brows furrowed as she was flummoxed, thinking about how she almost missed the boar. Turay looked at the boar thoughtfully and encouraged Hutia.

"You needed to aim just to the front of it so when it hears the string snap and starts to rush forward the arrow will still hit it in the middle through the heart."

Atabeira looked at her sister-friend and smiled with satisfaction.

"This is why we are a great team. Staging each other on the trail so no matter where it went someone would be able to get it. This was a great plan, Turay."

Hutia shook her black bangs from her eyes, her smile shone immediately through her almond eyes, as she replied.

"Frustrating! But we got food for the village."

"Ah yes, you are too hard on yourself sometimes. At least you still got it and thanks to you both, we have more food to share," said Turay smiling at Hutia and putting his hand on her shoulder.

He was at least a head taller than Hutia, almost three heads taller than Atabeira, and had grown into a fine young man. His patience was well-known, and he loved to teach his skills to whomever wanted to learn. When anyone asked him for help in honing hunting skills like archery, he always agreed without reservation. Since most of the men were forced to work in the mines, there was a shortage of food in the villages. Not many people were around to tend to the farming they needed to grow food. Everyone was trying to contribute in some way whether it was foraging or hunting for whatever food they could find and share with each other.

Turay smiled in appreciation at his friend whom he treated more like a sister, than a friend. He told the girls that next time it would be easier as working together requires practice and patience. He lashed the boar with his friends onto the staff he favored and stood up with Hutia to carry it back to the main village on their shoulders.

Even with them carrying the heavy boar, Atabeira had to half-jog to keep up with Turay and Hutia's long strides. Everyone teased her for being the shortest, but they all knew when it came to fighting hand to hand or using weapons, she was better than most. Hearing rustling in the brush nearby, she stopped for a moment and looked in that direction. The trio abruptly turned to look with an expectant smile growing on each of their faces when they realized who it was. Yukogueybana and

Gueriobanamu were animatedly talking and lumbering noisily towards them. Yuko had grown into one of the strongest young men in the area and his thick muscles flexed with every step. Guey was a head taller than Yuko with a lean frame that supported his speed and agility. Guey held up a string of four qúemi[24] he had gotten with his bow and arrows. He was grinning from ear to ear. His dark eyes shone brightly under his strong brow.

"Bei look at this! The qúemi were jumping out just to let me catch them," he announced happily.

"It was as if Yayael himself said, 'I know you didn't have good crops but here's this tasty qúemi and fruit to fill your bellies!'" Yuko replied, his deep voice was more animated than usual.

He was so happy that they would all be able to eat well this evening. Slinging the basket he was carrying to the ground he showed them the mangos, kenepas[25] and coconuts he was able to gather. Yuko looked forward to sitting by the fire and eating.

"You are always hungry," Hutia said as she giggled, happily.

"Well…" Atabeira replied while patting the boar presently on the ground, "we are all going to eat well."

Hutia looked at the line of rabbits and picked up one of its legs, and commented.

---

[24] Qúemi: Taíno word for "rabbit."

[25] Kenepas: a small seasonal fruit identified by a leathery green shell. It has a large pit covered in a peach colored pulp. Tart yet sweet in taste it only is ripe around the middle of the year.

"It's a nice fat one for sure; ooh maybe Bibi was able to make casabi."[26]

As they all walked to the village together through the lush forest, Atabeira couldn't help but feel a bit wistful. The abundant farming tracts her people had enjoyed for centuries was littered with dry crops. The areitos[27] were not as frequent as before and the numbers of people in the village were dwindling. The men were leaving to work in the mines, and many weren't returning. One by one the young women were being sent away or sent to marry the Spaniards.

The stories some would tell her filled her with alarm. Every time she asked her mother about the stories Bibi would reply, "Don't worry about it, focus on your lessons." And if she asked her father he would get angry and put an end to her questions. It seemed as if not one the elders wanted to discuss what was happening.

"Bei... Atabeira!" Hutia snapping her fingers in her ears spoke, "Hey, I was asking you if your father mentioned anything about the jeiticacu[28] coming soon?"

Hutia did not like the Spaniards at all and never hid her disdain from anyone. In her mind all her people's troubles began with their arrival. She never understood why the caciques and guazabara didn't kill them all years ago when they first arrived. Now it seemed to her, as if the leaders were all deferring to

---

[26] Casabi: bread made from the yuca root.

[27] Areitos: a festive gathering to celebrate an event or religious expression with song and dance. Usually characterized with mask wearing, music, and dance.

[28] Jeiticacu: another word of insult to the Taíno people.

the white faced buticaco and were afraid of them or trying to be more like them. Her face contorted in vivid disgust. Even though she was distracted, Bei answered her friend.

"He said soon. Agüeybaná is bringing ghosts to meet us and see our village after Juracan[29] is done having his way. I wonder if his liani[30] will come dressed like one of them?"

Agüeybaná was the cacique who controlled Borikén. Oromico, her father and Agüeybaná's cousin, deferred to Agüeybaná's directives. When the Spaniards arrived in their big canoas, Agüeybaná worked at getting to know them better. It was said that the Spaniards were invincible gods who couldn't be killed. Hutia really didn't believe that at all. He and his wives were all trying to show the Castilians that they weren't 'savages' at all by trying to teach them their people's ways and adopting some of theirs.

As the group walked together towards the village, they each took turns pairing up to carry the large boar so they wouldn't tire out too quickly. Atabeira was the shortest, so she carried the qúemi to compensate for not being tall enough to share equally the weight of the boar. She always felt awkward about it, but knew they all carried the weight in their own way. With a sigh in her heart, she reflected in silence on what was to come. The silence grew with every passing hill as the thought of the Spaniards arriving to their villages dampened their jovial mood.

---

[29] Juracan: the spirit of hurricanes. Hurricane season is typically towards the end of summer. Atabeira is referring to the upcoming hurricane season.

[30] Liani: Taíno word for "wife"

21

It used to be that some homes shared their food and some just cooked for themselves. Nowadays with the farming affected by the arrival of the Spaniards and their people coerced to help in mining, the villages shared every bit of food with each other. It was the only way to keep everyone fed and healthy. Still, Atabeira looked around at the village and her heart was glad that they all had each other. *At least we can still enjoy this together,* she thought as she chewed on the flavorful boar she helped to kill for the village. *Bibi knows exactly how to cook this perfectly,* she thought as she savored every morsel that she ate.

Yuko abruptly sat next to her, shoving his thick shoulder good-naturedly into hers. The fire pit roared with warmth before them as he smacked his lips. Looking at him, she saw him sucking the shells of a batch of cooked snails in one hand; with his other hand he held an open coconut.

"This is so good," he grunted in between mouthfuls. "You thirsty?" He offered the coconut water after he drank from it, his eyes open and smiling at Bei.

He loved her like a sister and was very protective of her. He knew she could take care of herself, but he still couldn't help looking out for her every chance he could. To him, she had that goodness of heart that one day could feel hurt through to her soul, and he hoped she never would feel that pain. He saw firsthand how the Spaniards were treating their people and he didn't want her to ever experience that. She was the twin of his soul and in his heart, he took that as fact.

"Wúa, natiao,"[31] she smiled at him gratefully holding up her gourd of water she was drinking. Looking at the flashing lights in the tree line she exclaimed, "Cucubano![32] Let's catch some!"

"Like when we were kids?" he asked incredulously.

"Come on, please?" she asked Yuko placing the drinking gourd on the ground.

Shrugging his big shoulders, he tossed the clean shells he had just finished eating into the firepit and followed her into the nearby field. Music started with the rhythms of drumbeats and the sounds of the guajey[33] filled the air in cadence, it seemed, with the coki.[34] Food and the smells of the cojiba[35] intermingled with the humid evening air. Fireflies glowed like stars shining in the grass and groves that surrounded them. Atabeira giggled happily as they tried to catch as many cucubanos as they could with their hands. They gently scooped them from the air as the dusk grew darker and the moon rose, only to keep their hands open and watch them lift in flight to the sky.

---

[31] Natiao: Taíno word for "brother"

[32] Cucubano: Taíno word for "large firefly"

[33] Guajey: Taíno word for an instrument made from the Guiro gourd fruit used like a scratching instrument

[34] Coki: Taíno word for a small tree frog commonly spelled as "coqui" in modern times. It sings a chirping sound mostly at night in a two or three note rhythm. "Ko-Ki" or "'Ko-Ko-Ki"

[35] Cojiba: Taíno word for a blend of tobacco commonly used in ceremonies.

"I need to tell you something, natiao," she walked slower as her eyes looked everywhere around her, but not his face.

She knew if she looked at him in the face, she was afraid she would burst out in tears. She avoided his gaze as the sky darkened and looked at the firefly resting on her hand. Yuko stopped walking realizing she was serious.

"What is it? What is wrong?" He asked in his deep voice knowing that something must have been troubling her to bring it up like this, away from their friends.

"Remember how I told you that Agüeybaná was coming right after Juracan leaves?" Her voice lowered, as she tried her best not to let it quiver. "He is bringing the Spaniard he wants me to marry with him. I am supposed to meet him and be spoken for by him."

Atabeira couldn't help but let the tears of fear flow silently down her cheeks. Yuko stared at her shadow form in the dark. It was as if he could feel her fear screaming from her body rebelling against the arrangement her father made.

"Wúa!" he said harshly. "Are you serious? Why you? Why not your sister? This isn't good. Wait, we can get you out of this right? We can talk to the group, and we can come up with a plan and..."

He rapidly fired off his thoughts so fast he didn't realize he stopped making sense.

"Yuko!" she spoke sharply to silence him in the moment.

He stopped, stunned. The feelings of a boulder on his soul started bearing down on him as he realized what exactly this meant and that no matter his good intentions, nothing would be done to stop it. If Atabeira refused it would mean certain death to all in the village. All the men would be forced into servitude and the women would be married off or raped and killed as sport. This was a no-win situation for her. It was her duty as the oldest daughter of the cacique to be married first to the Spaniards. That is what they wanted. An alliance between their people and the Spaniards. Agüeybaná gave in to them time and again. It was misguided but they were powerless to stop it.

"I had to tell you first. But I have to tell the others too. You know why I can't say no," her voice broke and her shoulders trembled with silent sobs; taking a deep breath, she let it out slowly trying to calm her emotions.

"What can I do to make it better?" he asked.

His own eyes filled with tears of anger. Oh, how he wanted to rage against this and shake sense into Oromico! But he knew right now, he had to go with what was happening.

Through her tears, Atabeira answered.

"I honestly don't know. Right now, I'm going to take it one day at a time. We still have the season until they show up. There's a lot of work we need to do to set up the village for when I leave. I don't know what's going to happen, but it will be good to try to make the best of it."

She dried her tear-streaked face with the back of her hands and wiped them with the edge of her new nagua. Looking down she thought how no one ever covered their chests. There was no shame to their bodies. She momentarily thought about how she heard about the Spanish women covering their bodies from neck to toes and thought they must be disfigured horribly to have to cover themselves completely. Hearing Yuko walk towards her closer she turned to him. Seeing the outline of his broad face looking at her with worry in the dark brought her back to the present moment. The sound of the music and festivities were getting louder. She knew the village would be sharing in mabí[36] and having fun.

"Come on, let's go back to the festivities. I don't want to miss anymore." Atabeira smiled through her dried tears as she took her brother's hands and started back towards the music.

"You need anything, you know..." his voice was gravelly and faded away.

"I know you are always beside me, my soul-twin," she smiled in response.

As they both walked slowly back to the festivities, Yuko couldn't help but feel the weight of dread from within. He knew she always had a second plan whenever they hunted. Once the group found out about what was to happen, they would have to come up with a backup plan in case things went wrong for the village, and Atabeira. Yuko took a deep breath of resolve while sitting off to the side as he watched Atabeira join the others in dancing with the music. He wasn't ready to pretend to be happy and join in yet. Her smile and laughter belying her fears, she danced with joy and abandon. One season of Juracan. That was all they had to prepare.

---

[36] Mabí: a fermented drink used in celebration

Dios mio,[37] *it is insufferably hot on this godforsaken island,* he thought to himself as he tugged at the collar of his camisa.[38] Pedro Hernández de la Garza wiped the sweat hanging on his strawberry blonde mustache and beard with his calloused hand. Years of working his way up in the ranks had transformed his pale skin into a tough shell with his hands rough from training with his espada y daga[39] daily. Ever since he was a niño[40] in Spain, he wanted the life of a soldier to be able to gain riches and retire in comfort. Not like his father who died a penniless artist. In his mind, he would do whatever it took to move up in status and comfort.

Even though he was only twenty-six years old, he was already a captain and was given the large responsibility of developing the resources to mine the island of San Juan Bautista.[41] Juan Ponce de Leon himself promoted Pedro on his last trip from Española, and gave him management oversight on the gold mining and growing tobacco fields near the namesake port of Ponce. His tall handsome frame was lean with muscle from

---

[37] Dios mio: Spanish for "my god"

[38] Camisa: Spanish word for a "long-sleeved shirt."

[39] Espada y Daga: Spanish for "sword and dagger"

[40] Niño: Spanish for "little boy"

[41] Puerto Rico was originally named San Juan Bautista by Christopher Columbus when they first invaded the island.

years of fighting under the weight of steel armor. He stopped in front of the well-polished mirror in his sitting room, one of the few nice homes built in the area and appraised himself with pride. *Not bad*, he thought as he looked back into his blue-green eyes reflected in the shine.

In the background behind him was the portrait of a stunning Spanish noblewoman sitting demurely on her chaise. He glanced at it in the mirror and turned spanning his open arms as if she were live in the room with him.

"¿Y qué, mi querida amor?" he gave a flourish of a bow.

He missed his wife, María Isabella. More frankly, he missed being the envy of every man who saw him with her. She was a stunning beauty, and the cousin of Juan Ponce de Leon himself. It was fortuitous that he was able to convince her he loved her, and that they should wed even though he was leaving for the islands. She was as ambitious as he was, and supported his goals in all ways. For that he was grateful, and knew he had to keep her happy lest it all dissolved in scandal if she left him.

He made a mental note to write her a love poem that evening so it would sail to her in Spain on the next ship. He turned abruptly at the sound of a soft knock on the door.

"What! Do none of these savages have any idea about timing?" he demanded sharply at the sight of the small copper skinned woman averting her eyes as she entered the room.

"Perdon, mi Capitán.[42] Capitán Rodriguez and Rey Agüeybaná have arrived for your meeting," she announced speaking softly, yet clearly in accented Spanish.

---

[42] Perdon, mi capitán: Spanish for "Forgive me, my captain"

She nervously kept her hands clasped at the skirt, but with her eyes not looking at him directly. This young woman was gifted to him by another don[43] to take care of his home for him. At first, she was resistant to learning Spanish, and how he liked his home kept. But a few lessons[44] taught her quickly how to be subservient and obedient. She still looked uncomfortable in the servant's clothing, but he was damned if he was going to let a savage care for his home naked.

"Yes, let them in and bring refreshments for them," he requested.

Pedro knew he had to maintain ties with the king of the indios[45] regardless of his personal distaste for them. After one last look in the mirror, he posed in the middle of the sitting room; smoothing his vest, waiting for his guests to enter.

The light wooden doors to the sitting room opened, and Capitán Rodriguez with Rey Agüeybaná strode in purposefully. While they were the same rank, Rodriguez was clearly older than El Capitán and very much overweight. The only reason he remained in a position of authority was a deference to his time serving the King and Queen of Spain. His fat belly pushed against his uniform jacket, made more uncomfortable because of the heat on the island. Agüeybaná, however, looked ridiculous to Pedro. It took all of Pedro's acting abilities to feign respect and admiration every time he looked the cacique of the island in the face.

---

[43] Don: the title given to landowners of the Spanish government

[44] The lessons referred to was actually physical, emotional and sexual abuse used to subjugate and control.

[45] Indio(s): Spanish word for "indian" Pedro is using the word as an insult and putdown on the aboriginal people of the island.

"Rey Juan Ponce de Leon, Capitán Rodriguez," he greeted with a warm smile and strong handshake with a nod.

Pedro knew he was appealing to Agüeybaná's sense of pride at adopting the name of his mentor and benefactor, Juan Ponce de Leon in the naming ceremony earlier in the year.

"What a privilege to have you both in my humble home. Please, sit. Rosio will bring us all refreshments," Pedro announced.

Dressed in a Spanish noble attire, Agüeybaná proudly wore the golden emblem traditionally marking his status as cacique on his chest over the Spanish clothing. His bronze skin was a stark contrast with the pale complexions of the men who were with him. The genuine trusting nature shone in his sparkling eyes, which crinkled in the corners when he shared his wide smile. Truly believing that being kind and generous to the Spaniards would benefit his people, he was easy to manipulate to do whatever the Spanish invaders wanted without using force. After all, the sheer amount of gold and resources would be much easier to seize without having any native pushback. And for some reason, they believed that the Spaniards were godlike and invincible.

Estúpido,[46] Pedro thought, *so stupid.*

Rosio quietly came into the room and served them refreshments. She was careful to stay just out of their sight, and not to cross in front of El Capitán. While serving Agüeybaná, she caught his eyes for a moment. Agüeybaná was taken aback at how dull and lifeless her eyes were when she looked at him. The dark circles under her eyes in direct

---

[46] Estúpido: Spanish for "stupid"

contrast to how she looked months ago when he saw her in her village with her family. Then she was always full of life and smiling. Here, all he saw was... empty. Her eyes were empty.

"Taíno-tí[47] Risanaiti," he said softly to her remembering her true name.

"Que Dios esté consigo, Rey,"[48] she responded in her heavily accented Spanish.

Agüeybaná nodded, shifting his eyes uncomfortably. She glanced apprehensively at El Capitán who smiled at the corners of his mouth. He was pleased she did not speak her native tongue.

"Well, Capitán," Agüeybaná forced a smile on his face and in his voice. "We have exciting news for you. My brother, Juan Ponce de Leon himself has requested that you are to be married to the daughter of a cacique I know north of here in the mountains. She is absolutely lovely and..."

Agüeybaná noticed the stunned look on Pedro's face, and inquired,

"Forgive me, you didn't know that was the plan?"

"Oh yes of course, you must have momentarily forgotten..." the old Capitán Rodriguez stammered. His blubbering would have been comical had it not been for the austere silence coming from Pedro.

---

[47] Taíno-tí: Taíno phrase meaning, "May the great spirit be with you." A common greeting among the people.

[48] Que Dios esté consigo, Rey.: Spanish for "May God be with you, King."

"Forgive me, Rey. I am merely impressed that you were able to arrange an auspicious union so soon. When am I to meet my lovely bride to be?" He inquired calmly through a clenched forced smile. He knew if Ponce requested it, then it was necessary for the mining to continue without interruption.

Rey Agüeybaná explained.

"After the hurricane season ends in a few months, we will travel north to the mountain regions. It is near where Guarionex has his territory. My cousin, Cacique Oromico keeps the area for me well. His eldest is promised to you after you meet, with your approval, of course."

Agüeybaná tilted his head towards the young capitán, continuing the explanation.

"She is a strong young woman from a good village. There's plenty of land in the area you can look to mine, and young people from the village to mine and work for our common goals."

Upon hearing the words 'mine' Pedro's eyes smiled.

"Ah, most auspicious indeed," he remarked. "It would be an honor and privilege to form an alliance with your cousin's village. I'm sure she will be a lovely bride. Please let me prepare my home for her, and we shall plan our trip so I can get to know this lovely beauty."

Pedro stood up from the chair indicating that their meeting was concluded and ushered them towards the door in the foyer.

"Yes, of course. If you have any questions, please ask," Rey Agüeybaná amiably stated.

Rey Agüeybaná and the older capitán said their goodbyes and left quickly. When they left, Pedro closed all of the doors behind him. Alone in the sitting room, he cursed loudly to himself. He was bothered that he had been caught off guard at the purpose of their visit. *Ay! To marry one of the savages. It is one thing to lay with them for fun but to marry? Ugh... You can do it Pedro,* he told himself. *If you want to be rich you will have to.*

As Agüeybaná walked away from the home of Capitán Pedro Hernández de la Garza, down the newly structured road. He couldn't help but feel as if he just made a deal with Maboyas[49] himself. The cacique quenched the rising dread in his heart by pretending to be interested in what the blubbering old capitán was saying about the benefits and virtues of an alliance through marriage. Deep in his soul, he felt disgusted. But he pushed all those feelings aside. *It's for the greater good. Whatever needs to be done to ensure we all are safe, and not at war; I will make sure it is done.*

---

[49] Maboyas is the Taíno diety/spirit for death and destruction

Atabeira had told their group about the arranged marriage shortly after she had told Yuko. True to form, the friends were angry at the circumstances Atabeira and their villages were forced to accept. The only way to keep the panic from welling was to plan for all contingencies. They talked about what would happen if the marriage were a good match, and what would happen if their worst fears became a reality. Turay was musing out loud about wanting to just take the village, and find someplace away from the invaders when Jaiba's face lit up.

"Guey! You remember where we used to sneak off to when we were little? It's about a day's walk from the west of your village." Jaiba's eyes were opened wide, and his grin looked like it could pop off his face.

"You mean the caves? Oh, the caves with the river! At the waterfalls?" Guey's face started to match Jaiba's as he realized the area he meant.

They had gone hiking when they were really little, leaving the village one day exploring and found a network of caves deep in the forest. It took them almost two days to get back home, and when they did their parents were none too happy thinking they were killed or hurt. Fortunately, he remembered the general area where they found safety for the night.

"Bibi almost killed you thinking you were dead." Turay's eyes crinkled remembering their mother's reaction to her missing son returning. Her relief had been palpable, but she made him promise never to go out exploring like that again.

"Yes," Guey chuckled. "I'm still her favorite though. But seriously, Jaiba that is a good idea. If we can find them again, we can set up an escape in case something goes wrong, and we need to leave the villages."

Jaiba nodded in agreement. The energy among the group was changing from dread to excitement. Now there was hope.

Hutia's brow furrowed, as they do when she is focused on a plan. Looking expectantly at Guey and Jaiba she asked,

"Could you find it again?" She glanced at Atabeira noticing that she was biting her bottom lip in nervous anticipation. *Bei is trying to not be too hopeful,* Hutia thought.

Guey and Jaiba looked at each other and grinned.

"It'll take a little bit of time, but we can all work together to scout it out and to set it up."

It took most of the season of Juracan with the friends breaking up weekly into teams and scout, while the others hunted. Halfway through the season in the middle of heavy winds and

rains, Jaiba and Hutia burst into Atabeira's bohio as Atabeira was making digo[50] with her mother and Anani.

"We found it! Bei we found it!" The pair stammered excitedly explaining that they found the caves and then stopped short realizing that Atabeira's Bibi and Anani were staring at them with a quizzical look on their faces.

"Uh... Uh...," they stammered.

Ari-Anani looked at them, her eyes narrowing. She treated all of them as if they were her children. It didn't matter how old they were or whose mother bore them. They were all hers in her heart.

"Tei-toca,"[51] she ordered.

"Atabeira, guárico guakia," Ari-Anani commanded.

Atabeira softly got up and walked to her mother and friends, looking at the ground in reverence to her mother. Bei knew when her mother spoke in that tone, she meant business. She was the younger version of her mother, petite, muscular with an animated face. Atabeira also knew when to push back when her mother demanded answers. Today was not going to be one of those days.

"Atabeira, explain," Bibi requested in her quiet but firm voice.

Atabeira began explaining.

---

[50] Digo: a type of soap made from plants that the Taíno used to bathe with. It was customary they would bathe daily sometimes multiple times a day to avoid sickness and infection.

[51] Tei-toca: Taíno for "Be still/quiet"

"Bibi, I respect you and Baba's arrangement for me to marry the Spaniard. But we are not children. We know what has been happening. In case something goes wrong, and our village is in danger we need a plan to keep you and all of us safe."

Atabeira looked at her mother, and continued the explanation.

"We have been searching, and Jaiba and Hutia finally found ... a safe place for us to go, in case things go badly."

Ari-Anani looked all of them in their eyes. One by one she held their chins. It was as if she could see into their souls.

"Han," she nodded as she spoke, "Taíno-tí au nanichi. Anani, guárico guakía."

Anani stood quietly and walked towards them. A few years younger than Atabeira, she was like Bei's little sister. Where Atabeira was strong and muscular, Anani was soft and delicate even though she was taller. Her plump cheeks retained its roundness of youth with her small eyes looking kindly on everyone in the bohio. Bibi had taken Anani in after her mother and father disappeared a few moon cycles before the season of Juracan came upon them. Anani was forever grateful and loyal to her spiritual mother, Ari-Anani; and took a part of her name in reverence to her in a guatiao.[52] Atabeira was protective of her sister knowing that she didn't have the same strength as the others in the group.

They all fell silent and glanced at each other nervously. Ari-Anani stood regally and smoothed her inagua as she looked at her youngest daughter.

---

[52] Guatiao: Taíno naming ceremony usually used in adoption of sibling or child.

"Anani, you are going to help me prepare for them what they need to keep us safe. But you may never speak of this to anyone else. The way to help them is to be discrete. This is our family, and we will help each other. Han-hán catú,"[53] Ari-Anani stated plainly.

Anani couldn't contain her smile, it came through her eyes, as she answered,

"I will Bibi."

Anani, loyal and grateful for having family again, turned to face the trio in front of her; and asked what they needed for the trip. They all grinned and started to talk softly about the provisions they would need in their safe caves.

The initial meeting with Capitán Pedro Hernández de la Garza was awkward at best. Oromico was strutting around the village proudly showing it off to the contingent of Spaniards with Agüeybaná. The kind monk, Padre[54] Tomás Del Rosario had been visiting for a month before Pedro and the contingent arrived; in order to prepare Atabeira for the meeting. Padre Tomás taught her the Spanish language and some Spanish customs. By the time the entourage arrived at the village she was already speaking Spanish with some fluency and learning

---

[53] Han-hán catú: Taíno for "Yes, let it be this way"

[54] Padre: Spanish for "Father"

how to read and write too. The Spanish custom of binding her chest, greatly annoyed her, at first.

"Why do I have to cover my chest? Is something wrong with it?" she asked.

"No, mi hija,"[55] Padre Tomás replied patiently. "You are perfect in God's eyes. But the Spanish people do not walk around exposed. It is against their customs and considered a sin under the eyes of God."

Everything he explained had a purpose under God's divine vision. To Atabeira, it seemed if it wasn't in alignment with the Spaniard's way of thinking then it was a sin to God.

"I don't like it," Atabeira frowned. She thought to herself, *Atabey and Yayael would never think we were wrong for being proud of how they made us.*

Nevertheless, she did as she was told to make her father happy, remembering that she was doing this for the greater good of her people. When she met her intended, she was struck at how tall he was and how golden he looked. It was easy to see why her people thought his people were god-like. He took her hand, gave a deep bow, and kissed her hand. Pedro's moustache and beard tickled her skin. She smiled amiably even though she could feel the glare from her friends as they watched from afar.

The visits were weekly, and they were getting to know each other. Pedro knew she hunted and remarked that she was very good at it when he arrived after a hunt and saw her catch the qúemi of the day. Catering to her likes he brought up his crossbow and taught her how to shoot it. She was

---

[55] Mi hija: Spanish for "my daughter"

surprised at how easy it was to use as she pulled the trigger. *This is supposed to be efficient?* She mused. *It takes forever to load. But its force is stronger than a regular bow and arrow.* Atabeira thanked him graciously every time he brought her something from Ponce or showed her something new. Even the Spanish fan that the women were so fond of carrying about she appreciated. *At least he's trying,* she thought to herself. *It could be worse.*

Her mother and friends were not amused by Capitán Pedro. They could see Atabeira was trying for their livelihood's sake, and would not intervene. But they could also see that something wasn't quite right with him. At one point, when Atabeira was trying on Pedro's heavy armor, almost falling over from the size and weight, Hutia turned to Ari-Anani and whispered angrily.

"You cannot see his soul in his eyes. Buticaco," she hissed in whisper glaring at him over her shoulder.

Ari-Anani saw her daughter laughing with the Spaniard and Padre Tomás over the armor which looked ridiculous on her small frame.

"Mhm," she grunted in reply nodding sharply.

Nothing else could be said. It was going to happen regardless of what they wanted. *Atabey guide her and protect her,* she thought to herself in prayer.

1509

The baskets, full of provisions, were laden with typical items needed for a home. Everyone carried a heavy load and weapons. They had been hiking up the mountainous regions, sometimes breaking freshly grown brush to get to where Jaibacovix was guiding them. It was a long and arduous hike with everything they were carrying. No one spoke much. They were too focused on the task at hand and time was of the essence. In a few days, Atabeira would marry, and they didn't know what would happen to the village.

The group was careful to cover their tracks as much as they could. They had been to the caves a few times already to scout them out. Turay and Guay stayed there a few days to make sure the Spaniards weren't coming around or that another village was using it. No one came around the desolate area. They marked the trail back inconspicuously with an agreed upon spot of where they had to look for the way to safety.

This was the last haul they would do together. A somber one at that. Atabeira had grown comfortable with the binding around her chest. To her amazement it wasn't too uncomfortable and kept her breasts from swinging when she hunted or ran. Hutia wasn't convinced at first but adopted it as well when she saw a benefit from it. But as soon as they were in their bohios they took them off and tossed the fabric on their hammocks.

Anani came with them on this trip bringing healing herbs and digo. She couldn't carry anything heavy, but she tried her hardest to keep up with them and not be a burden. Guay looked out for her all the time, staying with her so she would not walk alone and encouraging her along the way. Turay smiled to himself every time he caught Guay looking at Anani mesmerized. He knew his brother like he knew himself. She was the flower to his hummingbird. He was smitten and falling in love with her kind and gentle ways. Anani blushed every time she caught him looking at her with a dimpled smile.

Jaiba called over to Atabeira,

"Where are we?"

He was testing her to make sure she knew the way. If anything happened and they were separated they all needed to know how to get to safety. Atabeira paused for a moment and looked at the trees until she found the marker. She then exclaimed.

"Just over the bend we will be there."

"Han." Nodding his approval.

Jaiba was satisfied Bei knew what to do and how to get there. As they rounded the bend towards the waterfall, they followed the river until they came to the main veil of water crashing down. They looked up in awe at its beauty. Each and every time they came to the falls, they all said thanks to the spirits for this place. It was their haven and they were blessed to have it. Vines hung like wet hair throughout the rock faces and tree lines covering up their secret caves and tunnels.

There were two ways to get to the haven. Three, if one counted climbing up the vines themselves. The first way, was through the sharpest part of the rocks; on the bottom where the falls meet the river. If one was strong enough and able to withstand the power of the falls; then they could crawl under the veil to the path behind it leading up to the caves. Yuko, Guey and Jaiba had taken the time to carve a bit of a stepping plane so they could safely go up to the caves behind the lush branches and vines.

The second way was up the side of the falls; the boulders stood at the left of the falls. Additionally, tropical trees extended upwards, and partially concealed the enormous rocks; and then, halfway up the falls stood a ledge which, once on it a gap in the rock face was visible. Crawling the rock face revealed a ledge behind the main rumble of the falls. The ledge led directly to a tunnel and the tunnel led to the caves. The trees and vines concealed the caves. From all directions the great valley could be seen. The valley further revealed lush greenery and flowing rivers. The group was happy this place was theirs. Here, in this place, was plenty of food to hunt and, the caves would protect them.

The group waded into the water, careful not to leave any marks on the rocks on the edge of the riverbed. Guay held onto Anani's arm helping her wade towards the waterfall. The roar of the waterfall made it difficult to hear. Each person in the group, carefully turned their baskets toward the front of their bodies and waded deeper towards the sharp rocks guarding the cascading waterfall.

"Yuko, bring my basket please. I will help Anani get through." He asked his muscular brethren.

"Han-han," Yuko grunted with a wide grin. "No problem."

Anani looked at the water falls and saw one by one all her friends and sister disappear into the veil of water. Her eyes widened in fear as she drew closer to it.

"So how is this going to work?" she asked Guay.

"Do you trust me?" Guay asked looking in her eyes smiling at her.

"Yes, of course." She so wanted to be brave for him.

"Then when I tell you, hug me tight and hold your breath and whatever you do, don't let go. I will get us through it."

Already he could feel the rush of the water pushing against them; as Anani struggled to stay standing. She nodded and managed a brave smile. As they edged closer to the sharp rocks she clung to his muscular arm. They crossed the sharpest rocks carefully and Guay turned his face to Anani.

Guay yelled in her ear,

"Hug me!"

Anani wrapped her arms around his strong neck, and took a deep breath letting the rest of her body go limp. Her hands clamped hard on her own arms so she wouldn't lose her grip as she felt him drop into the cool waters. Guay encircled his left arm around her upper back, with his palm resting on her head making sure she didn't hit the rocks below; then he deftly kicked his feet to propel them forward using his free hand to pull through under the falls to the other side. She felt protected and safe despite her fear. Then she felt him push with his legs with all his might until they broke through to the surface and gasped for air.

"Are you okay?" he asked brushing her hair from her face as she gasped for air, and spit out the water.

She nodded yes even though she wasn't able to speak in the moment. Anani's round face filled with her smile as she chuckled, and realized that they made it to the other side. Blushing, because she was in awe of Guay, she was able to stand up in the pool and walk to the path. Guay helped her steady herself.

Atabeira was crouched on the edge grinning at the pair. She knew her sister was being brave and was proud of her. But she also knew something special was growing between Guay and Anani. Her heart was happy for them. Suddenly, a furry creature whimpered over to lick her hand, interrupting her thoughts.

"Opiel!" she cried out hugging the dog. "How are you nanichi? Are you hungry? We brought you treats."

The dog wagged its tail expectantly and knowingly. Opiel knew they all would give him a treat. He stopped when he saw Anani standing with Guay, and bared his teeth momentarily as a warning. Opiel did not know Anani.

"Tssk, she's my sister. You will love her." Atabeira spoke, as she took her sister's hand and brought it to the dog's snout petting his brown head softly. "See? She is one of us."

Satisfied the dog licked Anani's hand and went bounding up the path towards the caves.

"The spirits gave us Opiel to guard our caves when we are gone. He's all love. Don't show him fear, give him a treat every now and then; and he will be loyal to you." Atabeira explained to her little sister.

"Ah, he protects us like how Opiel Guabiron[56] protects Coabey,"[57] Anani remarked thoughtfully. "Maybe we should call this place Coabey?"

"Anani, sometimes you have the best ideas." Atabeira smiled at her sister. "Let's go so you can see what we've done."

There were five connected caves with five openings hidden from view. Tunnels within the caves were tight, but passable. The group had already brought up hammocks for resting, pottery for cooking, and other provisions in the last few months. Every week they would come separately or come together to prepare their refuge. It was small but the caves were deep, so more people could come if needed. Anani looked around in wonder at what they had already accomplished.

In each cave were sleeping mats with cloth, bows and arrows, daggers, spears and various tools. Pottery and baskets lined the edges of the caves. Flatware and bowls were set up near the fire area of the cave. Atabeira noticed appreciatively

---

[56] Opiel Guabiron is the half-dog, half-human keeper of the door to Coabey, the underworld. If your spirit was not good in this life, Opiel Guabiron would chase it away and not let it enter into Coabey.

[57] Coabey was the realm of the dead. Permission to enter was dependent on if you were good or evil in this life.

Anani appraising what was in the caves.

"You cannot light fire in the daytime or people will be able to see the smoke. Only at night." Atabeira informed Anani.

Anani nodded in agreement and walked over to the macana by Atabeira's sleeping mat. She reached out to it kneeling and stopped short of touching it; pausing to look at her sister questioningly.

Atabeira explained with resignation in her voice, "I cannot take it with me to Ponce. At least here it is safe for if, and when I may need it." Her little sister nodded that she understood.

Peeking out from the middle cave set up by Atabeira, Anani could see through the vines far and wide. She heard the sound of the waterfalls drowning their voices from the outside in. It was a perfect place to hide, to see without being seen. And unless someone saw how to get in, no one would be able to find them. Finished taking in the sights and sounds of the caves, Anani began setting up the herbs and medical supplies in the pots and baskets that were there. The group was going to spend the night in the cave, and return to the village in the morning. Soon Atabeira would be married to the Spaniard and everything would be different. Just how different, they couldn't foresee.

Padre Tomás Del Rosario sat in the bouncing wagon, on his way towards Atabeira's village. He was carrying the clothing Pedro sent for Atabeira to wear for their wedding. Pensively, he rubbed the large cross hanging around his neck with his thumb and forefinger, as he always did when he was in doubt. Knowing Pedro's reputation in Ponce, it was difficult for him to facilitate this union with the sweet Atabeira. The Padre mused, that even though she wasn't a Christian, he knew she was a good person whose soul could be salvaged through Jesus Christ. She was also smart and quick-witted. As he smoothed his greying beard with his hand, Padre Tomás smiled remembering how pleased she was in spelling her name on paper.

He sighed deeply and prayed,

"Heavenly Father, help me to guide the indios to know you. May they be protected and become saved through you, through Christ our Lord. May this union be blessed, and the village come to know you, Lord."

He prayed fervently, but still he held doubt in his mind on this union. *She is an innocent, and Pedro is the farthest thing from innocence.* All he ever wanted was to convert those to save their souls, as his soul had been saved through the Church. He rested his hands in prayer over his portly belly reciting the rosary as he thumbed through the beads one by one.

The wedding was unremarkable, Padre Tomás presided over the nuptials and Oromico affirmed the union. Contrary to village tradition, there was no celebration in the village; no areito, no music, no food for everyone. Just the service. Immediately after, Atabeira boarded the wagon with her husband to live in Ponce. When she arrived at her new home, she marveled at the size of it. Rosio was standing at the door ready to receive them.

"Rosio, this is your new doña. See to it she has proper clothes to wear so she is presentable." Pedro ordered.

It will take a lot of 'lessons' to teach this one how to be presentable indeed, he mused to himself. He knew he had to tread carefully, or he risked upsetting all their plans. Meanwhile, Atabeira looked at Rosio in confusion. She recognized her but couldn't place from where.

"Bienvenida doña," Rosio curtsied keeping her eyes averted to the ground.

"Taíno-tí ..." Atabeira started and was cut off immediately by her husband.

"In this house we only speak Spanish. I thought Padre Tomás explained that," he said sharply. The look on his face changed from amiable to disdain instantly.

"Perdoname, mi esposo,"[58] she replied.

Atabeira followed Rosio up the stairs to the dressing room adjoining what was to be her personal bedroom. There were clothes laid out for her on the bed. Not knowing how to dress herself in the Castilian attire Atabeira allowed Rosio to dress her. Rosio was working quietly and efficiently. Atabeira attempted to make small talk.

"How can anyone hunt in this?" she mused out loud.

"Spanish ladies do not hunt, princessa." Pedro replied softly from the doorway. "But you do look beautiful in the gown." *You look ridiculous,* he thought to himself. "Where are your shoes?"

"They hurt my feet," Atabeira said matter-of-factly. "I don't want them on."

"You must, you do not want to look like a savage," he replied without thinking.

"A savage? Are you serious?" Atabeira's defiance showed in anger at the insult to her people.

"WE are NOT savage. Point to me any Castilian who learns another language and adopts their culture in a few months! Show me any Spanish noble who even bothers to learn our customs and ways." Her eyes welled with pent up frustration. "You wanted to make this marriage happen to ally our village with the Spanish. Don't insult me in the process!"

Tears of anger made their way down her high cheekbones. She stopped what she was saying when she turned and

---

[58] Perdoname, mi esposo: Spanish for "Forgive me, my husband"

looked at him in the eyes; they were cold as his steel armor and emotionless.

"Rosio, vete. ¡Ahora!"[59] Rosio knew that tone of voice from El Capitán and quickly exited the room.

"You are what I say you are! As of today, you are my property and my wife, and you will do as I say!" he yelled as he grabbed Atabeira by the upper arms so forcefully, she thought her bone would snap. The fear was real as he growled over her, feeling the spittle coming out of his mouth in anger. It was in that moment she knew that he was capable of anything. The man who presented himself so amiably in her village was not the man she married. This she knew deep in her soul. His eyes were dead and flashed with madness at the same time.

What have I done... I've married Maboyas himself. Atabeira thought.

Music played jovially on the vihuela[60] filling the room with the plucking strings of a master artisan stationed in the corner

---

[59] Vete. ¡Ahora!: Spanish for "Leave, now!"

[60] The vihuela is a 15th-century fretted plucked Spanish string instrument, shaped like a guitar (figure-of-eight form) but tuned like a lute.

of the grand parlor. Spanish men, along with a few Spanish ladies and Taíno women dressed as Spanish ladies filled the room. Capitán Pedro Hernández de la Garza ensured a grand entrance for himself and his new bride. Received with the polite applause of their company, Atabeira took notice of all the people in the enormous room within her new home. Appraising the painting prominently displayed in the room while they were greeting their guests, Atabeira asked her husband who the Spanish lady was in the painting. His curt reply through his perfect smile cut her soul as much as his change in demeanor when they initially arrived.

"She is everything that you will never be."

Looking away from him to hide her hurt, she smiled kindly at the Spanish lady who sneered in revulsion back at her while fanning and whispering to another wife with a cackle in her voice. Atabeira smiled through clenched teeth. *The rude buticaco is lucky we are not outside,* she thought angrily to herself.

Throughout the rest of the evening, Capitán Pedro showed off his new acquisition, Atabeira, to the other dons of the region. Because the men were speaking so fast in Spanish, she was having a hard time following the conversation. A few words here and there were enough to cause deep resentment to anchor in her soul. *India, salvaje, tan joven, listo...*[61] their smiles didn't match their lustful gazes towards the small of her pinched waist. Pedro's firm grip around her arm was not in the genteel presentation he pretended it to be. She was his property and he made sure every man in the room knew that she was his, inclusive of whispers among themselves with

---

[61] India, salvaje, tan listo, joven: in Spanish it means "Indian, savage, so young, lucky". In this context it's expressed in a jealous manner.

laughter laced with ugly tones. The only men who looked at her kindly were Padre Tomás and Cacique Agüeybaná; both of whom showered her and El Capitán with kind words and blessings for a fruitful marriage. Neither daring to look into her eyes directly. In addition to the terse words and lustful stares, her feet were hurting terribly with the shoes Pedro forced her to wear. Atabeira could feel the blisters oozing into the shoes' starched fabric.

"I need a private place to go," she whispered quietly in Pedro's ear.

In response, he glared into her eyes for a moment, as if to see if she were lying. Motioning to Rosio he spoke to her sharply.

"Take her and help her."

Rosio curtsied and guided Atabeira to a small room in the back of the house. Placing a pot on the ground Rosio started to help Atabeira remove layers of underclothes so she could alleviate herself in the pot. As she took off the shoes, she couldn't help but notice the bloodied fluid in the toes of the shoes.

"Doña…" Rosio whispered kindly, "estas bien?"[62]

Wincing as she spread out her toes, Atabeira answered,

"Wúa, no se todavia."[63]

A look of sadness passed between them as Rosio nodded, barely containing her tears while cleaning Bei's broken skin. She knew all too well what Atabeira was married to and

---

[62] Estas bien: Spanish for "Are you okay?"

[63] No se todavia: Spanish for "I don't know yet."

wished quietly to herself that Atabeira had never walked into the home.

After all the guests had left, Pedro stayed in the parlor room enjoying yet another drink while, Atabeira was escorted by Rosio up to his bedroom to prepare for their marital responsibilities. *Marital duties with a savage,* he thought as he quickly downed another drink. *Mmmm, this always makes it easier.* Pouring himself another glassful, he looked at the portrait of his beautiful wife in Spain.

"Por la gloria de España!" he toasted drunkenly to the painting while wavering in his unbuttoned shirt.

Atabeira woke up the next morning to the sounds of roosters crowing sunrise. The fresh linens on the bed were wrapped around her generously. Where there should have been comfort instead, she felt tenderness in the cheek Pedro smacked with a backhand when she complained that he was hurting her. Bei could feel the bruise as the heat rose in her face from shame.

Bei noticed the pile of linens on the floor. She remembered that after he forced sex with her, he made her clean up the bloodied sheets.

"Well, I guess not all savages are putas[64] after all," he drunkenly sneered at the evidence of her virginity before he pitifully passed out on the bed.

I am the daughter of a cacique, a guazabara... and yet I let him shame me like this. Resentment continued to grow from within.

Rosio quietly opened the door without a sound and motioned for Atabeira to follow her out the door as she picked up the linens from the floor. Atabeira's feet were hurting badly from the damage done by the shoes. The pain of her feet didn't match the hurt she felt at the betrayal of her husband in his actions and his words. Walking silently, Rosio guided her into the dressing room and had Atabeira sit gingerly on a chaise.

"Princessa, estas bien?" she whispered softly.

Tears streamed down Atabeira's face. She felt like she could barely breathe with the ache she felt in her heart.

"Rosio, I didn't know..." Bei sobbed softly, afraid to wake El Capitán up. "It wasn't supposed to be like this." Despair welled within her. "I don't know what I should do."

The women finally looked in each other's eyes. They both understood that they both knew the demon they were facing.

---

[64] Putas: Spanish word for "sluts"

Silently, Rosio helped clean and change Atabeira into fresh clothing. Softly, she broke the silence.

"When he sees you today, and he asks you what happened to your face tell him you fell in the shoes. If you tell him it was his fault it will only be worse the next time."

Atabeira looked sharply at Rosio and grabbed her wrist to stop her from fussing with the clothing.

"How do you..." but before she could finish her sentence Rosio shifted her blouse to reveal bruising under her collar. Avoiding her gaze Rosio rested the hand on her small, rounded belly.

"Wúa... Does he know yet?" Atabeira asked realizing that the growing baby in Rosio was El Capitán's.

"No," replied Rosio in a voice barely above a whisper. "When he realizes he may kill me and the rest of my village. He will not want what he calls a half-breed with his name."

Atabeira felt a wave of nausea come over her. *Guakia Bibi Atabey, give me strength,* she prayed to herself.

"We will figure something out," she said with determination.

For the first time since Atabeira arrived at the house, Rosio wistfully smiled as she continued to help Atabeira get dressed.

Rey Agüeybaná and Padre Tomás walked together to pay a visit to El Capitán and his new bride. Discomfort filled the air and grew heavier with every step towards the grand home. No words needed to be said. They knew something wasn't quite right with El Capitán. Their fear of reprisal though outweighed their decency, and they embraced the unspoken rule to stay quiet about their concerns.

"May our Lord on high have mercy on my soul. May our Blessed Virgin guide and protect Atabeira in her marriage." Padre Tomás crossed himself as he walked and kissed his large cross before he and Rey Agüeybaná knocked on the wooden door.

Sitting down was so uncomfortable in the Castilian clothing, it took all of Atabeira's will to not groan in pain. The bleeding from the sex had stopped, but the healing from the physical and the emotional abuse she suffered at the hands of her husband made her feel shame. Conflicting thoughts raced through her mind, yet the safety of her village outweighed her personal safety and wellbeing. *How can I face my village, my mother, my father if I leave?*

Her conflicting thoughts continued. *El Capitán has no soul. Surely, he will take it out on my people.* She tried to consider possible outcomes; they all came to similar results. If she stayed, she knew she would end up dead. *Maybe not in body, but definitely my soul.* If she left, her people would then be at risk to be killed or worse, enslaved. At least if she returned to her village, she knew she could fight with them and help her people. Worst case scenario, she would die a physical death. Knowing the spirit of her family and friends in her village, she knew none of them would want this for her or themselves.

I will have to plan it out quickly, before the situation becomes worse for them, Atabeira finally concluded.

Rosio poured the strong café in the small cups for Atabeira, Padre Tomás and Cacique Agüeybaná. Padre Tomás looked at the darkening bruise on her cheek. As he reached out towards her face, he stopped just short of touching her.

"Princessa, did you have an accident?" he asked carefully. Rosio stopped pouring momentarily and looked at Atabeira quickly before resuming pouring the coffee.

"Si, Padre Tomás," she replied with a nervous giggle as she gently touched her face. "It is these shoes. I'm not accustomed to walking in them, and I tripped and hit my face on the door after the festivities last night."

Cacique Agüeybaná couldn't look her in the face, and kept his gaze on the chair. He felt intense shame and anger well up within himself. *I must follow the plan. Our lives depend on this.*

He truly believed if he conceded and facilitated the Spaniards to accept them that it would help their survival.

"You have a beautiful home here, Atabeira."

Her thinly veiled disgust was barely masked through her forced smile, as she spoke.

"Si, Rey. El Capitán's home is large. Not like our bohios though. I wish my Bibi and family would be able to visit with me here and be able to see all of this." Her unspoken thoughts raged, *and the lies you have told them.*

Agüeybaná cleared his throat uncomfortably, before he replied,

"Yes, well maybe one day we can make that happen."

He then looked at Rosio, noticing to her rounded belly, before looking away quickly.

Buticaco, Bei thought to herself as she gazed at Agüeybaná.

Padre Tomás looked between Atabeira, Agüeybaná and Rosio before speaking.

"Well, princessa, I am to go by your village tomorrow to visit with your father to tell him how wonderful last evening's festivities were, and how well you are adjusting to life here in Ponce. Is there any message you would like for me to tell him or your mother?"

Atabeira took a deep breath, pausing thoughtfully.

"Gracias, Padre Tomás. Please tell my mother that the Virgin Mary herself would not have been able to prepare a comparable Coabey as this home."

Excited to hear Atabeira refer to the Blessed Virgin Mary, Padre Tomás responded with genuine enthusiasm.

"¡Ah si princessa! It would be my honor to share your message with your mother. I'm sure she will be comforted in that you have embraced our Blessed Virgin Mary, and that you are happy in your new home here in Ponce."

Agüeybaná's face revealed his confusion, as he looked between Atabeira and the priest. Finally, he and Atabeira gazed at each other. It was then that he saw the resentment in her eyes as she looked straight into his; he also realized she was sending her mother a clear message. He stood up and extended his hand to hers in the Spaniard way. As he bowed to kiss her hand goodbye, he said in a warm voice,

"Taíno-tí Cacique Atabeira."

Padre Tomás, in his excitement over Atabeira's message, didn't even notice that Rey Agüeybaná was not speaking Spanish; and that he referred to the princessa as a leader would have been in the Taíno language. He stood up excitedly clasping her hand between his, and raising his left hand made the sign of the cross over her offering his blessings onto her and her home.

"Amen." He finished happily.

"Amen," she replied with a smile looking at Agüeybaná.

The message was clear, and it would not be intercepted.

Padre Tomás wrote in his journal; the date with the words on a fresh page. 'Today is a blessed day, for Princessa Atabeira referred to the Blessed Virgin Mary in her message to her mother. I can only hope that soon she will accept baptism, so her village will follow her example.' Once he offered a prayer of thanks to God and the Blessed Virgin, he summoned his carriage-driver to prepare for travels the next morning to Oromico's village.

The sound of the carriage bounding along the trail towards Oromico's village alerted villagers that a Spanish carriage was approaching. As the carriage continued into the village, Oromico walked by the batey arena forlornly. At this time no child played, yet he remembered how much he loved to watch Atabeira compete with her friends in games. Some of the older young people came out of their bohios to watch the carriage. A general uneasiness filled the air after Atabeira married. Mistrustful of the Spanish, the nervous villagers were prepared ready to fight or flee if needed.

Hutia came out of her small bohio, located close to the edge of the woods, and saw the carriage. Finishing hunting and carrying qúemi over his shoulder, Yuko heard the approaching carriage. He caught Hutia's eyes, as he jogged over to her.

"What's going on?" he asked.

"I don't know. It's the Spanish Priest's carriage though. Go get Ari-Anani. She needs to be there," Hutia answered.

"Han-han," he responded as he dropped the qúemi inside the door of Hutia's bohio. Yuko ran to Ari-Anani's bohio, at the other side of the village.

Eventually, the carriage pulled up to the cacique at the batey creating a cloud of red dust billowing around Oromico. Undaunted and unbothered by the dust cloud, Oromico stood waiting for the priest to step out of the carriage. The soldier protecting the carriage stepped down first from the carriage to help the overweight friar.

"Rey Oromico!" Padre Tomás exclaimed with joy in his voice, "How are you?"

"I am well Padre Tomás. Do you have news of my daughter? How is she?" Oromico asked in his heavily accented Spanish with a hint of worry in his voice.

"Ah, Princessa Atabeira is well in her big new home in Ponce. She was well received by all of society the night before last at the festivities. She looked like a proper Spanish lady of court," Padre Tomás bragged.

Ari-Anani walked in on the conversation purposefully, her regal presence causing Padre Tomás to pause in his babble in momentary awe of her bearing. Yuko was a few paces behind her. His muscular frame protective of the woman he considered to be another bibi in his life.

"Reina Ari-Anani, que Dios te bendiga siempre. I bring a message from la princessa for you," exclaimed Padre Tomás.

Ari-Anani nodded to him, giving him permission to share the message with her.

"La Princessa Atabeira is in a magnificent home with her husband, El Capitán Pedro Hernández de la Garza. She has been well received by polite society in Ponce. She wanted me to assure you with this message... she said, 'tell my mother that the Virgin Mary herself would not have been able to prepare a comparable Coabey as this home.' Isn't that wonderful?" Padre Tomás exclaimed expectantly to Ari-Anani.

Ari-Anani's eyes opened wide for a moment and then she composed herself.

"Gracias Padre Tomás," she answered graciously.

Ari-Anani glared quickly at her husband, turned away from Padre Tomás, and walked back to her bohio. Yuko did not understand most of the Spanish conversation, so he followed Atabeira's bibi back towards her bohio.

"Bibi Ari-Anani, what did he say... is she all right? Did you get a message? I heard her name mentioned." Yuko asked desperate for information.

"Tssk, tei-toca!" she admonished sharply under her breath.

Yuko stopped talking, but kept pace with her quick steps.

"Go get the others and bring them to me." Bibi Ari-Anani ordered.

Yuko's eyes never left her face as he nodded in assent. He left the bohio and ran to alert the others. As she stopped to look at her husband talking to the Spanish priest in the distance, she thought, *we must be ready for anything.*

Night after night, the same story would repeat. El Capitán would drink to excess. He would command her to wait for him in his bed. He would force himself on her, and then order her to leave. There was never any tenderness or kindness. There was none of the passion and joy her mother and friends told her it would be like. Once she tried to turn her face away while he was on top of her. He grabbed her face so hard forcing her to look at him, that she never turned it away again. The soreness between her legs became a constant reminder that to him, she was his property, and he would do with it whatever he wished.

During the daytime, if she remained quiet with a demure disposition, he was almost nice to her. Showing off the lands he claimed Juan Ponce de Leon himself had gifted to him, (*stolen from us*, she thought) Bei realized that she was learning what she needed to know to escape.

1. Guards posted at every entry around the fence and in the fields. It should take me about five seconds to run across that juncture, without these Castilian shoes.

2. Fire is always lit at the cooking pit in the servant's area.

3. Horses are kept tied in the stables. Two horses are tied to the back beam.

4. Every Spanish man has swords and daggers. Not one of our people in Ponce even has a macana.

Atabeira looked at the layout critically, mapping out possible escape routes and possible backup plans. She knew it would have to be done while he was sleeping in order to provide enough time before discovery. What she had to do was to figure out a way to help Rosio escape with her. No way would she let Rosio remain in that demon's home, especially pregnant. Rosio never brought up her pregnancy to Atabeira again after that morning. As Atabeira prepared and hoped for escape, Rosio kept moving about doing her job and hoping that one day, El Capitán and all the Spanish would magically go back to Spain.

Turay, Hutia and Yuko left for the two-day journey to refresh supplies in the caves of Coabey as they started to call them, shortly after the priest's visit. The others stayed behind in their respective villages. Should something happen, they all knew what they had to do. Run. Hide. Above all, fight to stay alive and get to the safety of the caves.

Uneasiness filled the air in the villages. Only the most trusted villagers knew about their plans. Some of their own villagers believed as Agüeybaná did, that if they were just nice and conciliatory that the Spanish would accept them, and all would live in harmony together. As each day passed the warriors knew with growing certainty that acceptance and harmony would never happen. They would have to be ready to fight or die.

Atabeira counted six days in her head. It would have to be soon. *I can't give him more opportunities or time to hurt me or my people.* Today was the sixth day. El Capitán had just left to go on his rounds, checking on the mines and the fields. Atabeira spoke to Rosio, in the kitchen.

"Rosio, I have a plan."

Rosio never turned around from wiping the table, but stopped moving.

"Risanaiti... please look at me. I have a plan." Atabeira beseeched in a soft voice, using Rosio's real name.

"No quiero saber."[65] Rosio spoke so softly, it was barely a whisper.

"Please, this can work. Please trust me. We need to talk about it while he is not here," Atabeira pleaded with a hurting heart.

---

[65] No quiero saber: Spanish for, "I don't want to know"

She wanted to help Rosio escape El Capitán, but it wouldn't work without her cooperation.

Rosio spun around with tears in her eyes, fear seemed to be yelling from every part of her being as she protectively placed her hand on her growing belly.

"If he finds out he will kill us both. You go save yourself, but I don't want to know. I can't help you," Rosio pleaded, her eyes showing fear and desperation.

"Maybe when he realizes that I'm pregnant he won't keep on hurting me. Maybe it will help our people." She stammered and clamped her hand over her own mouth. Not daring to even utter another word. Tears streaming down Rosio's drawn face.

Atabeira looked at her with bewilderment.

"Ris…," she began to plead.

"¡Mi nombre es Rosio![66]" she spat out in heavily accented Spanish. "My father made it clear I could not return or there would be shame and pain to our village. My name is Rosio."

She took a deep breath, shook her head in resignation, and said,

"The Spanish are here to stay. They aren't going away. This is my place. I have to stay. Los taínos no se levantarán de su control."[67]

She avoided Atabeira's gaze by drying a delicate coffee cup.

---

[66] ¡Mi nombre es Rosio!: Spanish for, "My name is Rosio!"

[67] Los taínos no se levantarán de su control: Spanish for, "The Taíno (Good Ones) will not rise from their control."

"Wúa!" Atabeira exclaimed in frustration reaching out for her arm. "¡Los taínos suben![68] We can fight him off together and get help. We can fight them all! We are worthy!"

"Wúa!" Rosio exclaimed angrily as she pulled her arm away from Atabeira.

Rosio pulled away so fast that the cup went flying across the room and crashed into many pieces on the ground. Its delicate porcelain features smashed into fragments.

"Don't bring this up again. I can't leave and I can't help you!" Rosio exclaimed as she dried her tears. Rosio began cleaning up the broken cup from the floor. "I won't help you," she said without looking up from her task.

Atabeira turned and quickly left the kitchen, walking gingerly up the stairs towards her dressing room. The pain in her feet, between her legs, were so minimal compared to the pain in her heart. She couldn't understand why Rosio wouldn't take this opportunity to leave. The fear she felt coming from Rosio was as palpable as the heat of the middle of the day. *I can't become like her. I have to leave. Tonight... Maybe if she sees I can get away she will change her mind and come with me...* Atabeira hoped it would be true.

El Capitán arrived late in the evening in a foul mood. One of the mines was not producing enough gold to cover what he

---

[68] Los taínos suben: Spanish/Taíno blended statement, "The Good Ones (Taíno) rise!

had promised Juan Ponce de Leon. It would not look good for him to not be able to produce what he promised. Atabeira sat quietly on the chaise in the parlor. She knew he would rather see her and know she was there. After all, in his mind, his property should be seen and admired.

The evening passed slowly. Every glass of wine he drank fueled his indignation and rage. At dusk Rosio lit the candles in the rooms in the house and presented dinner in the dining room to El Capitán and Atabeira sitting across from him.

"Atabeira, can you even cook?" he sneered at her.

Atabeira looked at him with confusion in her eyes.

"Cook, mi esposo?"

He laughed snidely, his once handsome face tilting with every word.

"Can... you ... cook?" Sarcasm dripped with every slurred word. "Oh wait, or do you eat all of your food raw like an animal?" Pausing for a deep breath, he said, "It is true then, not everyone was raised properly."

Atabeira looked down at her plate, heat rising in her face at his mockery of her. *Don't respond, Bei. It's not worth it. You have a plan. Stick to the plan.* Rosio stood silently in the shadows waiting to be of service.

Suddenly slamming his hand on the table, he yelled,

"Well?"

The force was so great the glass of wine tipped over spilling onto the tablecloth and onto the floor. While El Capitán raged, Rosio kept her head down not daring to move.

"¡Maldita!"[69] El Capitán's spittle was spraying of his mouth.

Atabeira jumped back into her chair. She was so scared she held her breath.

"Do you see what you did? ¡Estupida salvaje!" he barked. "¡Rosio limpia esto!"[70]

Rosio quickly moved to start cleaning the spilled wine.

"No, wait. It's your fault, you clean it up!" Pedro grabbed Atabeira by her hair in the back of her head and shoved her face into the wine on the floor.

Bracing herself so her face wouldn't get bashed in, he realized she was pushing back at him. Pulling her violently towards his side Bei stumbled as she cried out in pain. Rosio took one step towards them reaching out to Atabeira to help steady her. In one sweeping motion El Capitán backhanded Rosio into the wall behind them.

"Who told you to move?" he yelled at her. Rosio sobbed as she crouched down to protect her belly. "¡Basta! I'm in a house full of puta salvajes. ¡Mas animales de los negros!"[71]

In his drunken fueled rage, Pedro held both women in his grip; Atabeira by her twisted hair, and Rosio by the nape of her neck. He dragged them both up the stairs to his bedroom.

---

[69] Maldita: Spanish for "Damned"

[70] Limpia esto: Spanish for "Clean this"

[71] "Basta! I'm in a house full of puta salvajes. Mas animals de los negros!": Spanish words are translated "Enough! I'm in a house full of slut savages. More of an animal that the blacks!" In this context he is referring to the African slaves that Spain facilitated shipping to the Caribbean areas through the Atlantic Slave Trade.

Atabeira tried to help Rosio steady herself as she was being shoved into the wall, wanting to protect her and her baby from more harm. She could feel the hair ripping from her scalp with every twist and shove. Rosio's eyes flashed with such fear, that all she could do was try to protect her belly from the violent outbursts she was receiving.

When they got to his bedroom El Capitán shoved Rosio on the bed. Sobbing, she pushed herself as far back to the bedpost as she could and clung to it in terror. Atabeira gripped his hand that was latched onto her hair trying to pry his fingers off. When he noticed what she was trying to do he picked her up by her hair and punched her across her face in the very spot where the bruise was starting to heal. The room spun and everything was turning black. Atabeira couldn't hear a thing other than muted words. The blow to her face was with such force she couldn't move. She could feel her dress being ripped from her and being dragged onto the bed.

"Wúa," she barely uttered.

As she forced her eyes open, she saw Rosio starring at her in horror. Through the yelling she tried to focus her vision on Rosio. *I must help her. We have to get out. He's going to kill us.*

"Wúa," Atabeira said a little louder, feeling sensation again coming to her limbs.

Thrown on the bed, Atabeira grabbed the sheets with her fists trying to steady herself. El Capitán, in his drunken rage was taking off his dagger that he kept neatly in his waistband and threw it on the floor with his pants. Atabeira saw it as he was approaching Rosio who was whimpering in fear. Still trying to regain feeling, Bei mustered all she could to keep pulling herself inch by inch closer to the edge of the bed.

Suddenly, she heard Rosio yell loudly. As Pedro went to grab her, Rosio aimed her knee at his crotch.

He yelped and fell on the floor clutching himself in grimace and surprise. Atabeira pulled herself to the edge of the bed, *I need that dagger!* Rosio ran over to the open window on the other side of the bed away from the pile of clothes and dagger. Pedro, overcoming his shock yelled.

"Rosio! Stop!"

Rosio sobbed for a second, looked at Atabeira and said in a clear voice while clutching her belly,

"La taína sube!" as she flung herself over the edge.

Atabeira cried out,

"Wúa!" as Pedro stared in disbelief at the empty window.

"Capitán! Capitán! Come out! There's been an accident!"

Voices from the street were heard yelling up to the open window as Pedro realized exactly what had happened. He pulled on his pants.

"Stay here," he ordered Atabeira as he raced to go outside and dealt with the aftermath.

Wúa, she thought to herself as she watched him run out. Hearing his voice from the street she could only pick up a few words.

"Loca salvaje... problemas... busca al padre."[72]

---

[72] Loca salvaje... problemas... busca el padre: Spanish for, "crazy savage, problems, get the priest"

Atabeira pulled herself to the edge of the bed. Wincing in pain she looked and saw that in his haste Pedro forgot his dagger. *Now... the time is now. Han-hán catú.* Taking a deep breath, she mustered all her strength getting off the bed. Grabbing the dagger, Bei made her way to the door and down the stairs. Walking gingerly, she avoided the windows and the view of the growing crowd of Spanish and Taíno outside of the house. Everyone was busy towards the front of the house where Rosio had killed herself. Atabeira limped towards the back through the kitchen. *No one will pay attention to the back.*

She noticed the candelabra was close to the large painting of the Spanish lady. *And no one will notice me if they are focused on the house.* Quickly she shifted the heavy candelabra so that the candle's flames were on the thick frame surrounding the portrait. The roar of the flames lighting up the painting and seeping into the wooden frame of the house danced in the reflection of her eyes.

"Han, Risanaiti, la taína sube."

Making her way out the back of the house she stuck to the dark shadows. Glancing back only once to see the remainder of the demon house go up in flames, with muted sounds of the man she once considered her husband yelling her name repeatedly into the house. Looking towards the mountains where she knew her safety would be, she moved. Step by painful step. Reaching the back fence, she found the horses lashed to the post. As she touched the horse's neck, she exhaled deeply. Unlashing the horse from the fence she climbed up the post to help boost her onto the mare's back. The discomfort almost had her yelp in pain. Biting her lip, she tugged at the rope and made the clicking sound she heard the demon say when he was on horseback. With great relief

Atabeira rested on the mare's back as it turned towards the woods and the trails leading to her home.

Pedro Hernández de la Garza looked at his home burning to the ground in disbelief. Rosio's lifeless body was pulled off the fence she landed on and laid on the ground at his feet. Padre Tomás came rushing to his side, immediately knelt on the ground beside Rosio and started to administer rites. *This is all her fault,* Pedro thought to himself. *All this madness began with her and ends with her death here.*

"Capitán, donde esta la princessa?" the priest asked, looking frantically for Atabeira.

Never taking his eyes off the flames enveloping his precious home,

"En el infierno ," Pedro replied numbly.

Part 2: Yamocoa

1510

Opiel whimpered for a moment when he heard the steps but, relaxed when he heard the familiar whistle echoing through the caves.

"Ko-Ko-Ki."

Atabeira smiled at the sound as she tried to roll onto her feet from the mat where she was sleeping. *Oof, I'm getting too big for this.* She thought to herself. Feeling the jumping motion from one side of her belly, and the slow movement from the other side of her belly she rested her hands on each side and spoke soothingly.

"Shhh nanichi. It's okay. Food is coming." She chuckled to herself as she lovingly rubbed her enormous stomach.

It had been a long time since she actually even saw her feet and she was enjoying her peaceful pregnancy as much as she could. Turay and Yuko both popped their heads into the doorway of the cave. Both were bringing fresh fruit and cooked meat for her to eat.

"How's our favorite Bibi to be?" Turay greeted with a grin.

"I need help getting up," Atabeira responded with a half joking grimace holding out her hands to her friends.

As Yuko went to help her up, he exclaimed, "Bei, how many babies do you have in there? I think you got even bigger than the last time I saw you!"

Giggling she let them help her to the sitting stool near her mat. Looking at the fresh food they brought to her she was incredibly thankful and emotional at the same time.

"Thank you so much for helping me. I'm so grateful... and so are they," she tearfully thanked them. As she patted her belly she continued, "Bibi says it's just 2 in there. Some days it feels like ten. I think they may be ready to come out soon." Bei smiled lovingly at her belly while watching the babies stretching within her.

The night that she arrived at her mother's bohio she was wracked in pain and sobbing, eventually collapsing in her mother's arms. Ari-Anani sent Anani to get Yuko, Jaiba and Hutia. As they came in and saw her battered body, they were ready to go to Ponce to kill everyone on sight. Ari-Anani stopped their chatter.

"Tei-toca!" she commanded.

Looking at Hutia she told her,

"Get water from the river and then come help me and Anani clean her."

"Han," Hutia nodded running to get the water.

Yuko's eyes were red with anger and worry over his soul twin. Jaiba silently raged within at the injustice lying on the ground.

"Yuko, run and get fresh food and provisions from those we trust the most. I need you to make a carrier for us to take her to Coabey immediately. The Spaniards will be looking for her.

We have to get her out of here. Jaiba, run to Turay and Guay's village. One of them must help here, but have the other go with you to return the horse. Don't take the main roads but the back trails as fast as you can. They have to find the horse by the morning near Ponce," Ari-Anani urged.

Both young men nodded silently, turned and ran to complete their tasks.

"Anani, start packing all of the healing herbs and fresh wraps. Boil that for her to drink."

Anani dutifully took the herbs her Bibi motioned to and started to prepare the tea. Hutia returned with a fresh pot of water and knelt next to Ari-Anani. Ari-Anani ripped strips of fabric and dipped it in water and began to gently wipe the sweat, dirt and blood off of her daughter's face while Hutia held a cup to Atabeira's swollen lips to sip the tea. Tears were welling in her eyes as she cleaned her daughter while offering a prayer to Atabey for healing and strength. It was as if Ari-Anani was almost in a trance in her melodic rhythm and graceful movements.

Within hours, the remaining tatters of the Spanish clothing was thrown into the fire pit at the center of town. The mare was on her way back to Ponce with Guay and Jaiba. Anani was on her way with Yuko and Turay to bring Atabeira to Coabey. Since Hutia was the fastest runner, she stayed in the village, in case anything else happened; she could run for help, or stay and fight.

The first few weeks Atabeira was never left alone. While the physical injuries healed well, the anger and shame seemed to grow like a tree amongst the rocks. Reliving the trauma in her dreams fueled the rage and the rage grew. It seemed to have made her ill as everything she ate would be vomited up. Anani would look at her with a confused expression whenever that happened.

A month after arriving at the caves, Atabeira was washing herself in the waterfall when her mother and sister arrived escorted by Jaiba. Happy to see her up and about, Ari-Anani embraced her daughter with joy. As they pressed each other's foreheads together in a loving greeting, Ari-Anani looked into her daughter's eyes and gasped. Cupping Bei's face with her right hand over where the bruise used to be,

"Taíno-tí nanichi... Atabey has blessed you."

Atabeira looked at Bibi in confusion. Ari-Anani took Atabeira's right hand and placed it over her belly.

"You are Atabey's legacy. This is why you have been sick. It may not have been what you wanted. But they will be here before Juracan returns for his season again. And like our great Atabey, you will raise them yourself. Han-hán catú."

Atabeira, her sister Anani, and Jaiba, all stared at Ari-Anani in disbelief. And just as serenely as she announced the impending births, Ari-Anani turned to walk up the walkway towards Atabeira's cave.

The heat was magnified by the humidity, as the sun climbed through the sky over the trees.

"Ay nanichis, settle down for a bit and come out soon. I can't wait to see you." Atabeira spoke in warm, soft tones to her unborn babies within her.

She usually passed the days like this - bathing in the pool behind the waterfall. Talking to her babies. There was not much to set up for their arrival as Anani and Ari-Anani provided all that was needed for a safe delivery and care for the newborns. Their friends took turns spending the night with Bibi Ari-Anani, Anani and Atabeira to ensure they would be protected from the Spaniards or any other dangers.

For now, the Spaniards believed that Atabeira was dead. Oromico didn't know that his daughter was alive though. Because he collaborated with Agüeybaná, Ari-Anani made the decision to hold back until the time was right and Atabeira could protect herself. Until then, Atabeira and her babies would be a guarded secret. In the meantime, Ari-Anani and Anani told Oromico they were gone to tend to a pregnant woman in a village who needed help and support during a difficult pregnancy. Oromico, always distracted since the wedding, hesitantly nodded his support, while looking longingly at the batey area that was now void of all joy and festivity.

Atabeira exhaled audibly as she paused grabbing her lower belly mid-waddle towards the opening of her cave.

"Oosss," she groaned and her face grimaced as the skin across her belly and back tightened in a strong contraction. Anani, weaving a basket stopped and jumped up to help Atabeira.

"Ahh! Ooss," whimpered Atabeira as she grabbed Anani's shoulder.

Doubling over in pain from another contraction as her water broke, it poured out of her splashing on the cave floor. Inhaling sharply at the sight of the water, she looked into Anani's eyes in a panic.

"Get Bibi!" Atabeira eked out through a contraction.

"Yuko! Yuko!" Anani yelled.

For the first time, Anani's voice carried loudly through the air. Yuko, by the waterfall, was able to hear it over the roar of the water crashing on the rocks. Leaping up over the steps to the walkway he made it to the cave opening in time for the next big contraction to hit.

"Agh," Atabeira groaned softly.

This contraction made Atabeira's knees buckle. Yuko jumped to Atabeira's side just before her knees hit the ground. He could see the contraction squeeze her skin and the outline of her babies pressed against her tight belly.

"Help me get her to the mat," Anani directed.

As they brought Atabeira to the mat, Anani gathered blankets to cushion her back against the wall and to support her propped up knees.

"Go quickly and get Bibi and Turay," Anani ordered, "They went to the grove of trees by the last sign to get some herbs."

"Han." Yuko answered as he pressed his forehead to Bei's, "I will be right back with Bibi."

Atabeira nodded and managed a smile while controlling her breathing as Yuko ran out the cave.

Meanwhile, Anani quickly brought out all the herbs and the bundles of fabric they would need for the delivery. She had everything laid out and ready for Ari-Anani to use. Once she finished preparing the delivery materials, she focused on Atabeira and checked on the babies. One baby was already a challenge, but two babies proved to be even more difficult. Although the risks were great, helping Atabeira and checking on the babies, Anani worked as if she were commanded by the spirits themselves. Anani helped Bei move forward, in order to massage her back and to hum the breathing rhythm.

"Ooo-Ooo."

The breathing rhythm, actually more like a melody, hummed from the essence of life itself. The sounds came from a place of comfort and love - radiating calm and peace in the cave. Pretty soon, Atabeira was entranced by the rhythm and the humming. She started to hum the melody with Anani, and they both rocked through the contractions, painful though they were.

Ari-Anani calmly walked into the cave, pleased to see that all was ready and that Anani had done exactly as she had taught her to do. She turned to Turay and Yuko who were standing in the doorway. Lying next to Atabeira's mat, Opiel watched and whimpered.

"My sons, cover the opening and stay nearby. We may need your help," instructed Ari-Anani.

She then turned to the herbs and started combining what was needed. She applied compresses to Atabeira's sweaty brow, and hummed the melody along with Anani and Bei.

"Drink nanichi. You need your strength," cajoled Ari-Anani; continuing to move with purpose.

Hours passed as the sun roared with a red glow while Turay and Yuko remained steadfast in their watch; listening for when they were needed. Bibi Ari-Anani and Anani massaged with every contraction, hummed with every breath, until Atabeira announced she needed to push.

Growling and howling like a wild animal, Atabeira pushed her firstborn out. Anani looked at him with wide eyes listening to his strong cry of first breath. Ari-Anani held the baby up for Atabeira to take and hold. Bei took him from Bibi and wept openly. She kissed his bloodied brow and wiped his head with the cloth she was gripping. A momentary confusion came over her face when she realized his hair was the red color of the sun. Her eyes met his and her heart filled with peace knowing that his wise brown eyes mirrored her fighting soul.

"Makagüeybaná," she said his name softly, "he will be the great big sun."

Ari-Anani looked at her grandson and nodded,

"Han-hán catú nanichi."

Turning towards the cave opening she yelled,

"Turay! Yuko! Guárico guakía!"

They lifted the cloth at the door timidly. The moon was rising, and the sun had just set.

"It is good. The great Atabey has blessed us. We need your help," Ari-Anani pleaded.

It was not common for them to be present for births, but as it has been, the unorthodox way always seemed to work out for them.

"Yuko, you must hold onto the baby and keep him warm," Ari-Anani said, as she handed the baby to Yuko; who looked a bit awkward at holding the newborn swaddled in his muscular arms.

"Turay, I need your help," continued Ari-Anani.

Turay nodded and went next to Atabeira where Bibi indicated.

"Nanichi, the baby is facing the wrong way. We must turn him around for you to be able to help him breathe his first breath." Ari-Anani explained to her daughter.

A look of panic came over Atabeira's face as her eyes moved from her firstborn held by Yuko, to her mother, to Turay. As Turay took her bloodied hand and looked into her eyes, he encouraged Atabeira.

"You can do this guazabara. Atabey is with you. We are with you."

Bei nodded.

"Han-han," she said with conviction.

With Anani supporting Atabeira from behind, Ari-Anani and Turay went about massaging her belly to turn the baby's head down. The pain for Atabeira was excruciating. She howled and grunted through every movement, every painful massage until...

"Now, you must push now," Bibi announced.

With a guttural howl from Atabeira, blood flowed with the birth of her second son. Bei held her breath, as she couldn't hear him cry like his brother.

"What's wrong? Why isn't he crying?" she asked.

She held her breath with fear. Ari-Anani massaged him vigorously reciting incantations to Atabey and Yayael. Then, a boisterous cry erupted from the second newborn as well as his brother.

"Ja!" They all laughed through their tears.

Emotion filled Turay's face as he looked in awe at Atabeira. Pressing his forehead to hers, he whispered.

"Guazabara Bibi!"

The second newborn was placed on her chest, and she wiped the blood from his thick black hair. To Bei, his big brown eyes seemed to hold the answers to the universe. As she kissed his brow, she whispered breathlessly.

"Makarayabaná, you will be as the great big moon in the sky."

The love she felt for her sons in that moment was like no other feeling in the world. Soft chatter and joy enveloped the cave as they cleaned. Atabeira prepared to nurse the twins.

"Daca-abibi,"[73] Atabeira tiredly said with awe.

---

[73] Daca-abibi: Taíno for "I am a mother"

Ari-Anani gazed upon her daughter and prayed silently to herself, *Atabey, you have my daughter as your legacy. And like you, she now has her sons.*[74] *Guide and protect them always.*

Capitán Pedro Hernández de la Garza was at his desk in his new home built on top of the old site. It was grander than the one before but all the luxury he surrounded himself with didn't ease his soul. The bitterness within him grew every day. His disgust for the indios was more and more evident every week when he toured the mines and fields, and reviewed his accounts with his foreman, Javier. Javier had spread out on the table papers and accounts to show to El Capitán, his lean frame leaning over the table as he motioned to the documents. Javier did not look at El Capitán directly.

"Capitán, the mines and fields will not meet the quotas you have directed," he said matter-of-factly.

As Pedro drank from his glass, he angrily asked.

"And why not? I can't let Juan Ponce de Leon down. This is ridiculous."

"You don't have enough people to mine and tend to the harvests in the volume you are requesting." Javier answered timidly.

---

[74] In Taíno Mythology, the great Atabey was the mother of twin sons, whom she raised by herself.

The empty space where his teeth used to be on the sides of his mouth gave his already thin Castilian face a gaunt appearance. Resting his hand on his peppered beard, Javier's sharp eyes darted across the charts. Knowing better than to try convincing El Capitán to reduce the quotas to manageable numbers, he tried to think of a way to ease the captain's anger.

"You need more manpower," Javier suggested.

"Maldito indios. Never enough. And where, pray tell, do we pull indios from... the sky? Can't we just have them work more?" Retorted the frustrated El Capitán.

"The ones who are surviving the current pace and work would probably get sick and die as the others have. The indios are not the healthiest when it comes to this kind of work. Our resources are starting to dwindle as they are dying off or running away. I recommend that we go the route of Hispanola and start bringing over the negros to work here. But that will cost money to purchase them," Javier gently advised.

"Before we start spending more, what villages still have resources for us to use?" Pedro asked as he pushed papers around his desk. "What about the villages from the mountain region? Have they provided enough men for our work?"

"Oromico won't send anymore." Javier stated uncomfortably.

"I already know they haven't. Lazy salvajes. Ever since that bitch died, he's been unreasonable and not sending men to work," retorted Pedro. "Well, out of respect for his daughter we haven't pushed for what is ours. However, we can no longer be conciliatory since we have quotas to fill. Don't we, Don Javier?" Pedro asked snidely.

"Si, Capitán," answered Javier.

"If they won't give us the men to work, we will have to convince them that it is in their best interests and make them accept the work," continued El Capitán.

Taking a deep satisfying breath, drinking from his glass, and then turning to the lean man standing before him, El Capitán spoke, "We will have a meeting with all of my lieutenants tomorrow at noon. We will plan it all out then and convince these little savages that it is never in the best interests of los indios to avoid their due responsibility to Spain!"

Atabeira woke with a start, sweat soaking into the sheets and mat she where she rested. She checked on the babies, lying next to her in their baskets. A full moon cycle had passed since their arrival. They were growing quickly and getting chubby, as healthy babies should. The redheaded twin, whom she nicknamed Ris[75] was forever hungry and nursed around the clock. The twin with black hair she nicknamed Rai,[76] would nurse a large amount at one sitting, and then sleep peacefully for hours. Atabeira routinely woke with overwhelming panic and dread, because of her nightmares. With her mother and Anani back in the village, she worried about their safety away

---

[75] Ris: Taíno word for "red"

[76] Rai: abbreviated version of Karaya, the Taíno word for "moon"

from the caves. Because she knew what evil El Capitán was capable of doing, she feared for the wellbeing of her people

Unable to fall back asleep, she quietly arose, picked up her macana and the dagger she always kept under her mat. Smiling at the light shining off them, she spoke to her weapons.

"Hello datiao."[77]

The moonlight brightened the dark cave as the sun started to rise, the melodic singing of the coki permeated the veil of vines protecting the caves.

"It is time we get to work again, isn't it?" *Strike… thrust… block… Oh how I've missed this,* mused Atabeira.

El Capitán inspected the brigade. Soldiers lined up for inspection with their pikes[78] and halberds.[79] The sharpened axes and spikes glinted in the sunlight. The men sweat profusely under their armor and leather botas. While it was a ridiculous amount of weight to carry in the humidity on the

---

[77] Datiao: Taíno word for "my friend"

[78] Pikes: spears commonly used by infantry

[79] Halberds: hatchet commonly used by infantry

island, it did offer protection from simple weapons that could be used in battle. The armor and leather botas would easily deflect the indios' tools. *Good,* thought Pedro to himself. *This is good.* From his white Andalusian mare, El Capitán towered over the Castilian men he commanded.

"Were we able to replenish our supply for the crossbows?" He asked his lieutenant who was walking next to the mare.

"Si, Capitán." The lieutenant answering as he turned toward the troops.

"¡Presentan armas!"[80] the lieutenant bellowed.

In response to the order, every soldier proudly presented their weapons in synchrony. *We are ready,* El Capitán thought to himself smiling gleefully.

"We march before dawn," he announced to the lieutenant.

"Si, Capitán," answered the lieutenant.

Padre Tomás del Rosario moved away from the window, as he watched El Capitán turn down the road towards his newly built home. Guilt wracked the soul of Padre Tomás. Prostrating himself on the ground, holding his large cross in his hands; he prayed fervently for guidance.

---

[80] Presentan armas: Spanish for "present arms"

"They are innocents. This isn't right. He will kill them all. I must do the right thing." He knew he couldn't ask for a carriage or he would look suspicious. "With our Father Lord and Blessed Virgin Mary beside me, I must tell Rey Agüeybaná," Padre Tomás concluded to himself.

"María! Please come here," he asked of his servant.

Of all the Spaniards, she was fortunate to have a kind priest to serve; instead of one of the soldiers. The petite woman donning servants clothing answered him kindly,

"Si, Padre?"

"I will be out for a long while. After I minister to some of those in need, I will be using some time to reflect and meditate on the will of the Lord. Please do not wait up for me," briefed Padre Tomás.

"Si, Padre," she bowed her head reverently. "Que Dios esté consigo."

"Amen," Padre Tomás responded while crossing himself. *I will need Him, more than ever before.*

Walking towards Agüeybaná's village area situated on the outskirts of Ponce, Padre Tomás felt an overwhelming sense of dread. Notorious for his strict discipline and cruelty, the area was under the supervision of Don Diego Salcedo, who had just returned from another excursion to Hispaniola. Everywhere he went the indios were convinced he was a god and could not be killed. They lived in fear of his cruelty and retribution.

It took more than most of the day to reach Agüeybaná's yucayeque[81] of Guayanilla. To the left of the caney longhouse was the beginnings of a large home of the same style as the Spaniards. It had been abandoned to rebuild El Capitán's home and had not been touched since. Padre Tomás approached the longhouse timidly announcing his arrival.

"Rey Agüeybaná, I'm sorry to disturb you but please, I must speak with you."

Padre Tomás was stunned to be greeted at the doorway by the mother of Rey Agüeybaná instead. Doña Ines, as the queen was baptized, looked distracted with tear-stained face. He knew her well as he had administered the rites of confession to her in the past.

"Doña Ines! What is wrong? Where is Rey Agüeybaná?" He asked with genuine concern.

"Mi hijo... nanichi... the great sun...," wailing she crumbled into Padre Tomás' arms, her frail body trembling in angst.

Padre Tomás looked in the longhouse as he held the bereft woman in his arms. Agüeybaná's wife wept kneeling beside his motionless body on the Spanish style bed that seemed misplaced within the longhouse.

"¡Ay Dios mio!" Padre Tomás, crossing himself, realized that his hope in helping Oromico died with him.

"Por favor, Padre Tomás. You must give him last rites. He must go to heaven!" Doña Ines had a wild look in her eyes.

"Si, si," answered Padre Tomás, as he walked with her towards the bed to administer the rites.

---

[81] Yucayeque: Taíno word for "village"

Torn within himself, he began the liturgical rites. *May the Heavenly Father, Virgin Mother and Holy Spirit forgive me.*

Oromico turned away from the opening of Ari-Anani's bohio and turned towards his queen. The year had not been kind to him, his greying hair glistened in the light of the fire. Disappointment was evident in his voice, but tears of joy in his eyes.

"She's alive? And has sons?" Oromico asked as his hands trembled at the news.

"Yes, Oromico. I'm sorry we didn't tell you. It was my choice. We couldn't risk Maboyas himself to come and kill her, and all of us." Ari-Anani's spoke simply and clearly.

Ari-Anani's heart was devoid of emotion for her husband, because the man she had loved was no longer there; yet she hoped some spark of who he was would return.

"You were right. You have always been right," his deep voice quivered.

Full of guilt, Oromico covered his face as he spoke through his fingers.

"This is all my fault. All my fault."

Ari-Anani was overcome with compassion for Oromico, as she spoke to him.

"My íro,[82] please come back to me. To us. To our people. We must fight against the buticaco ghosts! Please."

She pleaded as she hugged him with all her might, burying her face in his chest willing him to rise to be the man she knew him to be. Embracing her in return, as he kissed the top of her head; Oromico whispered into her hair,

"Han-hán catú liani."

Ari-Anani looked into his eyes, and saw the man she loved. Breaking from the embrace for a moment, she went to the opening of her bohio. Shutting the cover to her doorway she looked at her husband with genuine love again. Taking his hands, she led him to her mat by the fire. For the first time in many years, Oromico and Ari-Anani felt the love and passion they once had again just as the first of the rains started to fall on their village.

Anani was on her way back to the bohio when she saw the opening covered. Quizzically, she leaned in and listened for a moment in the rain. Realizing what was happening, she giggled and turned away towards her cousin's bohio around the bend. *It's about time,* she smiled to herself.

---

[82] Íro: Taíno for "man" or "spirit of a man"

The rains fell as Juracan opened the heavens and tried to wash the Spaniard infantry away. The demon himself stayed on his mare impervious to the strong winds and pelting rain.

"Por la gloria de España!" El Capitán bellowed over the howl of the winds, commanding the army to destroy all within their sight.

Their orders were very clear: capture all the young men and women, crush everything in their sight, and what was not to be captured was to be destroyed. Scores of infantrymen rained upon each bohio in teams. Screams could be heard from all directions. The old were being hacked with the axes. The young broken into submission. Violence crashed through the walls of the bohios on the unsuspecting families nestled in their mats sleeping around the fires. Terror filled their hearts looking at the ghost-like appearances of the infantrymen, that came to take their very souls. Ari-Anani was the first to hear the screams.

"Wúa! This isn't a dream!" She yelled as she shook Oromico awake.

They both looked in each other's eyes in terror. Just as they were moving to get their weapons, the opening to the bohio crashed open with most of the wall. Pedro rode into the home on his mare, flanked by soldiers on foot with crossbows. His own Toledo sword pointed at them.

"What are you doing?" Oromico demanded as rage filled his eyes.

"Taking what you refused to give me," Pedro replied with derision.

"You will never have what wasn't yours to begin with," sneered Oromico, knowing that no matter what, Atabeira and his grandsons were safe, and Pedro would never know the truth.

Incensed that even in the face of certain death, Oromico wouldn't cower to him, Pedro raged and swung his sword slicing the cacique's throat wide open.

"Wúa!" yelled Ari-Anani catching him as he fell and trying to stop the bleeding.

Husband and wife looked into each other's eyes, she watched his life spirit leave his body. Rage filled her with such power, she took her husband's manaya[83] and went after Pedro - hell bent on killing him on the spot. Alas, the soldier who was beside him quickly took aim and shot her through the heart with the crossbow. Feeling the piercing of the arrow in her heart, Ari-Anani fell back on Oromico; her lifeless body over his. Immediately, Pedro ordered the soldiers,

"Rip all the gold off of them and set this whole damned place on fire."

---

[83] Manaya: Taíno word for "hatchet"

Anani awoke to soldiers bursting through the opening and the walls. Screaming in fear, she and her little cousins cowered near the pottery at the back of the bohio. Despite the fear, Anani tried to push some of her cousins out of an opening against the back wall.

"Wúa! Wúaaaaa!" Anani and the cousins screamed, as the soldiers grabbed the girls and dragged them out, tying their wrists together behind their backs.

The soldiers dragged the boys out for inspection. If they were old enough to work on the mines, the soldiers tied them up in another group. If they were too young to work, they killed them with the spears and axes on the spot.

Anani held onto her little cousin as tight as she could, and tried to fight the horde of soldiers off them. The soldiers managed to rip one of her cousins from her arms, and they tied her arms together. Sobbing, she screamed for help. One of the soldiers came close to her, and she remembered what she could do. She used all her strength and kicked one of the demons right between his legs. His response was to punch her square in the middle of her face. She heard the crack of her nose and felt the blood gushing down her face. As she was being pummeled around her face, arms and legs; she couldn't understand what the Spaniards were saying as she lost consciousness.

"Maldita india! Déjala que se muere!"[84]

Hutia and Jaiba were the farthest away in their small bohio on the hill opposite to Ari-Anani's bohio. After quickly getting their weapons, they made their way to the brush-line to see what was happening. The people of the village were running in as many directions as they could trying to get away from the demons attacking them. All who tried to escape were swiftly killed with the crossbow, or mercilessly pinned to the ground with the spear to die an agonizing death. Making their way closer to the fight, they knew that if they were caught, it meant they would be killed on the spot. Hutia and Jaiba tried to keep out of sight of the soldiers.

Hutia was the first to see what was happening in Ari-Anani's bohio.

"Jaiba..." Hutia whispered as she grabbed his arm, staring in horror as the soldier lifted his crossbow and killed Ari-Anani. Hutia tried to get up and go to them.

Jumping up, Jaiba grabbed her and covered her mouth muffling her screams, as they hid in the tall grass.

"Wúa! We can't help them now!" he said as he cradled her on the ground. They sobbed quietly in the rain, as they

---

[84] Déjala que se muere: Spanish for "Leave her, she will die"

watched the flames engulf the homes and consume the lives of those whom they loved.

The rains continued to pour over them, as they desperately tried to think of a way to help.

"Anani!" Jaiba whispered. He was the first to see her body thrown onto the pile of dead bodies.

Anani's body was one of the few without a spear in it. Hutia and Jaiba lying low, crawled in the tall reeds to get closer. Hunkering down they saw one of the infantry looking around for any survivors, pulling the spears from the limp bodies. Inching closer to Anani's cousin's burning bohio they saw movement and a flash of copper in the grass. Anani's young cousin, Mabodomaca, lay face down in the grass, his arms covering his head. Slowly Jaiba and Hutia slid their way to him.

"Mabo," Jaiba whispered to him. "Mabo, can you run?"

Recognizing the voice, Mabo peeked out from under his arms and nodded.

"Do you know how to get to Guey and Turay's village?" Jaiba continued to ask.

The boy glanced over to the woods and nodded. The rains started coming down harder, thankfully deafening any noise. Jaiba took the boy's arm and made him look in his eyes.

"You need to warn them the ghosts are coming to kill them all. Do you understand? Can you be brave?" Jaiba asked Mabo.

Shivering in the rain, Mabo took a deep breath and nodded.

"You are the fastest runner. Slide slowly until you get to the woods. When you get past the second trees you run. You run as fast as you can until you get to Guey or Turay. Tell them to get everyone to safety and meet us at Coabey. Can you do that?" asked Jaiba, looking at him with hope.

"It's your turn to be a guazabara and warn them. You don't stop until you find them, and you get them to safety. Okay?"

Jaiba grabbed the boy and pressed his forehead to his, saying,

"Taíno-tí guazabara."

Mabo nodded and went to the treeline slowly and steadily. Turning away from him, Hutia and Jaiba started inching their way closer to the pile of bodies. Above them, heavens opened in a roar of wind and rain pelting the Spaniards sideways. The trees bent to the winds. It appeared that the spirits were showing their anger at the desecration of their people.

Just as quickly as the Spaniards pounced and eviscerated the village, they left. The conquistadors forced the ones they captured to move with them back down the road towards Ponce, tied like animals, ropes around their throats, hands and feet.

Once Hutia could see the Spaniards were out of view, they crawled towards the pile of bodies left behind. There they saw Anani tossed on the side of the pile. Her naked body bloodied and battered. Kneeling beside the pile, Hutia and Jaiba went to check her for signs of life.

"Anani," Hutia cried out her name. "Please, please breathe. Anani... please..."

Blood dripped out the corner of her mouth as she gurgled, moaned and moved her hand.

"Jaiba, help me move her to the edge of the woods over there," Hutia pleaded.

Jaiba picked Anani up carefully and easily, carrying her swiftly while Hutia checked the other bodies. Seeing that there were no other survivors in the pile she quickly joined Jaiba and Anani, by the tree. As she got closer to Jaiba she could hear him talking to her so softly as he held Anani with his back leaning against the tree shielding them as the rain let up.

"Little sister, hold on. I'm here. Hutia's here. We're going to take you to Coabey, and you will be okay."

Tears streaming down his face he brushed her hair from her face, begging his sister-friend.

"Please forgive me. I'm sorry I wasn't there for you. Please… be okay."

Looking at her broken nose he sobbed as he cradled her in his big arms. Jaiba looked up at Hutia hoping for good news, he asked,

"Anyone?"

Hutia shook her head, and answered.

"Wúa."

Jaiba stood up with Anani in his arms. And together they started the trek towards Coabey in silence.

The rains had come and Atabeira woke to the clap of thunder and lightning. She couldn't breathe right and didn't know why. In a panic she checked on the babies and saw they were resting in their baskets beside her. She walked over to Yuko sleeping on a mat on the other side of the cave and woke him up.

"Yuko. Yuko. Something is wrong. Wake up," she whispered as she pushed on his shoulder.

"Wha-? What's wrong? Are you okay?" Yuko stammered as he woke.

"Yuko, something is wrong. I feel it. Go to the village and please check on them," she pleaded, feeling something was wrong and trusting her instincts.

"Okay," he agreed and prepared to go.

He trusted Atabeira, and if she said something was wrong, he knew better than to question it. Opening the doorway flap keeping the rains out of the cave he looked out and cursed.

"Bei!" exclaimed Yuko, hands over his mouth.

He could see past the trees towards the village. Where the village used to be, fire and smoke were rising along with the ominous clouds and hurricane. As Atabeira looked past the trees with him, she clutched her stomach and knelt on the ground. Opiel whimpered beside her.

103

Numbly she whispered,

"It's begun."

Refusing to let her go, Jaiba carried Anani the entire journey to Coabey, only stopping for food, water and a little bit of rest. The entire day through the night until the next morning they walked in a steady pace. Longing to get to safety and help Anani, they spoke to her in soft voices talking about funny things that happened in the past, telling her how brave and good she was and how much they loved her. She never responded, but remained unconscious for the entire journey.

As they approached the second to last marker on the trail, Hutia heard a rustling sound behind them. Hiding behind the brush on the trail, Hutia held her trusty manaya in her hand, ready to kill all who threatened them. Jaiba kept hold of Anani, not letting her go, his body tense ready to defend themselves.

"Turay!" Hutia exclaimed when she saw him walking in front of the trio.

"Hutia!" Turay replied over-joyed seeing his sister-friend.

Turay was walking with Guay and little Mabo was between them. She sprinted to them, with tears in her eyes, and embraced them all. She noticed that Mabo had a macana of his own in his hands. It looked like the one that Guay had when he was little. Jaiba came out from the brush holding Anani in his arms. Turay and Guay looked at his face, and then Anani. Anger showing in their eyes as they wiped away their tears. Mabo cried out,

"Anani!" and ran to hold her hand.

Looking up at Jaiba with his big brown eyes welling with tears, he asked.

"Is she..."

Interrupting Mabo and putting her hand on his little shoulders, Hutia assured him.

"She is sleeping and hurt. We are taking her with us so she can get well again."

Mabo held her limp hand and pressed it to his forehead, pleadingly saying.

"Anani, you saved me Anani. I listened to you, and you saved me. You stay sleeping, I will take care of you now."

Guay walked up to Jaiba and without saying a word stretched out his arms. Jaiba gently passed Anani to him. Guay cradled her and kissed her matted hair gently whispering.

"I'm here. I'm never letting you go. You are my flower."

Walking in the direction of Coabey, Mabo wouldn't let go of her hand as Guay carried her towards safety. Jaiba held back and bit his lip to keep from crying. His arms were cramped, and the emotional exhaustion overtook him for a moment.

"Turay, they are gone. We couldn't do anything. They are all gone," said Jaiba.

Hutia hugged him to her and let him cry.

"Nanichi, if it wasn't for you, we wouldn't be here either," she replied gently.

"Your village?" She looked at Turay hopefully.

Turay didn't take his eyes from his brother in arms, and answered,

"Mabo made it in time. They all scattered and went to different villages to the north and east away from here. Your choice saved many."

He could feel the guilt in Jaiba; compassion and gratitude filled his voice as he spoke.

"Datiao..." putting his hand on Jaiba's shoulder, "Natiao... You did the right thing. Thank you."

Jaiba took a deep breath, composed himself, and stated strongly.

"Let's go. We must get Anani safe. And we have to figure out what we are going to do next. The ghosts... jeiticacú... we have work to do."

Using the litter they made for Atabeira a long time ago, they tied rope and lifted Anani to the caves. Over the next few days, they mourned over their losses, honored their dead, and set themselves up. Yuko and Turay made the journey back to the village to double check for any possible survivors while the others tended to Anani and to the babies.

A few days later, after another round of heavy rains, Yuko and Turay returned carrying a little girl. Her almond eyes peeked out from under her bangs as she sucked on two fingers for comfort, clutching Yuko around his thick neck. The waters were too rough for her to swim through the waterfall, so they lifted her using the litter while the men climbed up the side of the cliff using a rope that was thrown down to them. When Mabo saw the little girl, he cried out.

"Tínima!" and picked up his little sister in a great hug.

She squealed with joy. Yuko grinned as he spoke,

"Anani saved her too. We found her hiding under a log by the big tree near their bohio. You remember it Atabeira? We used to play hide and seek there." Bei smiled wistfully at the memory.

Anani was initially in and out of consciousness, but continued healing slowly over the next few weeks. Guay wouldn't leave her side feeding her sips of herbs and tea, while crushing fruit and meat so it would be easier for her to chew and swallow. Hutia and Atabeira cautiously bathed her; carefully washing her hair every day. They knew keeping her clean would help her heal faster physically. Her button nose was crooked in the bridge, but the swelling and bruising was starting to heal. When she slept the nightmares would come and she would wake up screaming. Guay was there to comfort her every time. At first Anani would stay in Atabeira's cave. After a few weeks, she was walking around and playing with the young ones a bit.

Anani chose to move to Guay's cave with the children. She felt safe with Guay and wanted to be with him. His patience with her healing helped seal their love for each other.

Part 3: Ganocum

Towards the end of Juracan season, Turay asked for them all to meet in Atabeira's cave. It was the biggest cave among all of theirs. The little ones played with the babies cooing in the back. Opiel romped with the kids letting them pet him and pull at his tail. He guarded them and loved letting them rest their heads on his lean body as they napped. The fire burned with warmth in the cool evening air. The song of the coki was clear despite the roar of the waterfall. The group looked at each other as they sat in a circle. Turay looked at them all thoughtfully as he spoke.

"I think it would be good if we talked about what this is going to look like. We can't hide away forever. This we know for a fact. We have witnessed firsthand their intentions are not good."

Pain registered momentarily on his face, as he informed them,

"The ghosts are never going to leave."

Atabeira looked around at all their faces. No longer children she felt a deep love and attachment to them all. They weren't just friends. They were all a family now. A yucayeques of their own borne of a lifetime of relationships, experiences, and solidarity.

"I want to fight," she announced with conviction.

"Han-han, it's time," agreed Yuko. They all nodded in agreement.

"Do we have contact with any of the other yucayeques?" Jaiba asked.

As Turay took out a stick and started pinpointing a rough map, he spoke.

"We should reach out to them and set up a system. We can't do this alone. The ghosts are strong and will have to be hit from different areas."

"Can they be killed?" Anani's soft voice rang clear. Her eyes looking at Atabeira directly.

"Yes... They are like us. But they are hard to kill," Atabeira responded carefully, adding, "Güeybaná has taken over. He thinks more like us. I think we should reach out to him first."

"He's over by Añasco last I heard, staying with Cacique Urayoán," Turey informed them.

Turay looked up from his makeshift map, and asked,

"Who should go?"

Atabeira looking determined, answered,

"I will go. Anani, will you take care of the twins for me for a few days?"

"Han-hán catú," Anani smiled thoughtfully as she answered

"Just as Bibi would have said," Atabeira thought aloud.

Yuko looked at Atabeira.

"I'm going with you. There is no way you are going alone."

Turay nodded, "I'm going too."

"Han-han, would you stay and protect our children and our home?" Atabeira looked at the rest of the guazabara sitting beside each other.

"You can count on us," Hutia replied.

As the planning for the journey began, excitement and hope enveloped the cave like a warm blanket, soothing their fears. So much was at stake, but they were determined to fight back against the invaders. *Los Taínos suben,* Atabeira thought to herself.

The meeting with Güeybaná was fruitful. When he realized who Atabeira was, he immediately greeted her as family. His strong features reflected intelligence and kindness. One could only imagine the look of determination that would cross his face in battle. Looking at her with an incredulous expression on his face, he spoke.

"Cacique,[85] we thought you were dead! Atabey's legacy is true!"

---

[85] Cacique: as the sole surviving member of the matrilineal lineage of her village, she inherited the title and all the honors with it. The term Cacica to refer to the feminine was interpreted by the Spaniards who insisted on gender-based roles in titles.

The Good One Rises (La Taína Sube)

"I am risking a great deal coming to see you Cacique," Atabeira looked at him, speaking with sincerity. "Thank you for meeting with us unannounced. We want to fight beside you and the rest of our people who are done with what the buticaco ghosts are doing to our people and our land. We want to stand beside Agüeybaná the Brave."[86]

Güeybaná took a deep breath, his large muscles flexed at the mention of fighting. Light shone in his eyes, he then invited the unannounced visitors to sit with him. Guiding them into the caney they saw Cacique Urayoán sitting on a dujo[87] speaking to some of his people sharing news from Ponce; he listened intently to what the people were telling him. Each wore a golden guanín on their chest indicating their status as leadership, with Güeybaná's being larger and more ornate than Urayoán's. Atabeira recognized it as the one she saw before when his brother was cacique. Güeybaná whispered into Urayoán's ear. Looking at the trio standing before them with wide eyes, he nodded and asked the people with whom he was conversing to leave and to return later in the evening.

"Cacique Atabeira, we are honored you and your guazabara are willing to join the fight. Please sit and let us discuss," said Urayoán; as he motioned for someone to bring out a dujo for her to sit on, and a ture for Turay and Yuko, each.

Turning to the left of her, Atabeira spoke.

"Turay, tell them your ideas."

---

[86] When Agüeybaná died, Güeybaná took over the title of head Cacique of the island, as well as Agüeybaná's name. He was a relative of Agüeybaná. However, he was known as Agüeybaná the Brave as he resisted the oppression forced by the Spaniards.

[87] Dujo: a bench reserved for leaders and dignitaries

Turay took a stick and started drawing a diagram in the dirt floor, while telling the survivors his ideas.

"It would be good for us to develop a communication system; an alert, as well as a call to arms. Utilizing the peaks of the mountains, we could strategically signal each other using the conch to amplify with codes set up of sounds. If we can have reliable runners who can do this, it would save time and protect our villages from possible discovery."

The kings looked at Turay's plan thoughtfully, and nodded in agreement. Turay continued.

"We can plan attacks and alert each other for timing, as well as if we can move forward or abort. By collaborating we can save the lives of our people and disrupt the Spaniards."

"Where is your village located now?" Urayoán asked.

"That is not for anyone to know," Yuko plainly stated, "We have six guazabara who have trained since infancy together. We mobilize and move quietly, efficiently, and effectively. All you have to say is when and where."

"Do your guazabara always speak like this?" asked Urayoán, looking at Atabeira, his face registered shock by the answer.

"When they speak, I am speaking. Where I go, they go. We stand beside each other. Han-han catú," answered Atabeira.

Channeling the regal bearing of her mother, she embodied the confidence of a warrior and leader. The caciques looked at each other and nodded to Atabeira in assent.

"We just received word from Ponce that a collaborator has agreed for his daughter to serve a don. They will send a contingent of soldiers to retrieve her from her father's village north of where your father's yucayeques was located. It is near Toa. They would have to pass through your father's lands to get to her and return to Ponce."

Urayoán stopped speaking and looked back and forth at Güeybaná and Atabeira.

"Can your guazabara take care of them?"

Atabeira answered as she looked at Turay and Yuko, both nodding in agreement.

"Yes, consider it done. When are they to pass?"

Discussing the details of the plan, Atabeira hoped that the pounding of her heart would not be heard by the caciques. *This is what needs to be done. They cannot get away with their evil ways.*

Returning to Coabey took a day longer than needed because they decided to double back and hide, making sure they weren't being followed by a scout. The waters were almost back to normal, so they were able to get to the caves from the waterfalls again. When the babies saw Atabeira they both smiled and squealed with glee. She immediately kissed them all over their heads as they crawled onto her lap. Loosening her binding, the babies nursed while everyone was debriefed. Watching everyone eating together, laughing, and planning out their mission while the kids played, this was the happiest

Mynet Velez

Atabeira felt in a long while. She looked to her babies sleeping with their heads on Opiel nearby and she couldn't help but smile. Turning back to the circle where everyone was chatting and eating, she noticed Turay staring at her with a smile on his face.

"What?" she asked self-consciously.

"I haven't seen you smile like that in a long time. You look happy," he hesitated to bite his food, "and beautiful."

Anani was feeding Tínima and happened to catch Atabeira blushing a deep shade of red just as Turay looked down at his food. *This is good,* she thought. *We can all use joy and love in our lives.* She turned towards Guay looking at him teaching Mabo how to strike with his macana. He caught her gaze and gave her a dimpled grin. She smiled back at him with genuine love in her smile. *This is how it should always be.*

A few ambushes on western trails away from their yucayeques netted them a few good daggers, Spanish goods, and weapons. They examined the few pieces of armor they brought and eventually practiced moving while wearing them. They all agreed that the heavy metal was counterproductive to their style of fighting and movement. Keeping it at the caves, Yuko kept examining it for how it could be modified for their needs.

117

The timeline approached faster than they imagined, intending to stop the contingent from reaching the collaborator's village. Everyone prepared to be gone for a week, and began saying their goodbyes. Anani was comfortable staying behind with the kids, for she felt safe with the protection of the waterfall, and the dagger that Guay gave her. Guay, Hutia and the others really took their time teaching Anani little by little the foundations of fighting. Mabo had been hard at his lessons with Guay, whom he called Baba. Guay looked at him with pride and pressed their foreheads together. Mabo clutched his macana with pride.

"I will help Bibi take care of us all Baba."

Embracing Anani right before he went under the waterfall, Guay looked at her and whispered,

"Taíno-tí nanichi."

Anani, Mabo, and Opiel stood on the uppermost ledge to watch them enter the forest. As they disappeared one by one, covering their tracks from the stream Anani and Mabo stood until they were all gone. Then they turned towards the big cave to settle in for the week without the rest of their family.

Atabeira perched herself on the mid-level branch in the middle of the rainforest's tree. Her dark eyes glared into the

dusk scanning for any and all movement on the ground. She adjusted her bare feet on the branch to maintain her balance while her nagua flowed with her movement. Her dagger strapped to her leg in its sheath in case she needed it. Softening her breathing, listening for harsh steps that the ghosts made recklessly. Red and black body paint helped to conceal them all among the branches. She heard the crunching of the botas, followed by the unmistakable whistle from Jaiba in the south,

"Ko-Ki! Ko-Ko-Ko-Ki!"

Atabeira's heartbeat roared in her ears. Her breath deepened with every crunch she heard. The now familiar Castilian words in chatter coming from the invaders who were oblivious to the pack above their very heads. She was in the middle of the pack within the trees. Hutia was just ahead of her, Turay on the other side of the trail across from her, and Yuko just behind him. The first series of whistles was to warn they entered the area. The small contingent walked through not noticing that the animals in the forest weren't making any sounds. *Not today evil ones... not today.* She waited for the signal from the north side of the trail from Guay.

"Ko-Ko-Ko-Ki! Ko-Ki!"

She grinned ready to pounce on the soldiers below.

"JAAAAAA!"

She roared at the top of her lungs, leaping from the branch as she swung her macana to the soldier's open face. The entire contingent looked up in horror to see the fury of copper, red and black raining from above. The soldier Bei struck fell to ground unconscious instantly as the macana bashed his face in. A swift second blow put him quickly out of his misery.

Guay ran south on the trail towards the first soldier; who, dressed fully in his armor, was trying to run. Using the spear, the soldier stopped and squared off with Guay ready to fight, skillfully wielding the spear to sweep Guay's feet. Guay wore no armor and was able to jump nimbly, clearing the spear. Before landing on the ground Guay smashed his macana over the top of the helmet crashing the soldier's head into his chest. The Spaniard collapsed in a heap on the ground, as Guay turned heading south to help the others.

Looking around quickly, Bei saw Hutia strike another Spaniard in his strong arm with her manaya. His strong arm was rendered useless to wield the crossbow he held in his hand. The arrow discharged into the ground, barely missing Hutia. Swinging the manaya with all her might, Hutia landed an upward swing knocking his metal helmet off his head, sending most of his lower jaw with it across the trail.

Coming in from the west, Turay arched his new machete like he always trained with it in his hands. Striking at the knees in graceful motions he disabled the Spaniard closest to him. With a loud crack, Atabeira whaled his back forcing him on his knees with her macana. Turay was able to spear the machete in the leather space between the front armor and back armor plate, slicing him open from the collarbone to the jaw.

Yuko leaped from where he was hiding landing squarely in front of the soldier that was coming up from the rear. With a fierce growl he used his battle axe as a battering ram right in the soldier's face. Jaiba ran up just in time to send his macana crashing at the back of the Spaniard's head. In less than two minutes, the entire Spanish contingent was dead.

Catching their breath, they looked around and nodded as Bei caught Turay's gaze. Atabey was with them after all. Knowing this was only a small battle won, there passed a look of understanding of what this win meant for their people. As they headed back towards the rest of their family in Coabey, they fell silent in the knowledge of one thing they knew for sure... *Los Taínos suben.*

Book 2 ~ Excerpt of the La Taína Series:

The Good One Keeps Rising

(La Taína Sigue Subiendo)

<u>1511</u>

Packing her gowns into trunks, María Isabella's handmaiden chatted with her doña.

"Doña, what do you think it will be like in Ponce? I heard it was very warm there. I shall pack for you the summer clothes and a few garments in case it gets cold at night," the cheerful handmaiden chattered.

"Si, Josefina. Gracias," she spoke absentmindedly.

Her fine aristocratic features softened in the pale glow of the candlelight. Reading the letters from her husband, María Isabella was troubled. The letters were becoming increasingly shorter, and less frequent. She had heard that the mines weren't producing as much as her cousin, Juan Ponce de Leon had hoped. Her large hazel eyes, rimmed with long black lashes read, and re-read the letters. *Yes, something wasn't right.*

María Isabella's beautiful face darkened a bit with a scowl, as her eyebrow arched reflecting on her handsome, yet inconsistent husband. She knew she married someone who wasn't as high status as she was, but her ambition recognized that her cousin, Juan Ponce de Leon dismissed a great deal of Pedro's shortcomings because Pedro was so loyal to him. Pedro was her ticket to remain in high social status amongst all the pretty belongings she craved to have around her.

"Josefina, please pack some of the jewelry that mi esposo, El Capitán, graciously gave me for our engagement and wedding... And, of course, the gowns that match them," the Doña requested.

"Si, Doña María Isabella," Josefina answered,

Upon hearing the tinkling of the bells announcing the arrival of guests, María Isabella rose from the writing desk and appeared to glide across the room to the hallway. She walked softly down the expansive staircase to greet her guests. As the Doña entered the grand sitting room, two high ranking gentlemen from the military quickly stood to pay respects to the lady of the manor.

"Doña María Isabella, as always, your beauty is unmatched," the general bowed kissing her emerald ring on her hand.

His gallantry reflected a testament to his reverence to her, and her family's status. As his large, well-groomed moustache tickled her soft hands, she smiled at him as if he were the only man in the room.

"General Marquez," she spoke as if she were singing in a breathy voice. "I am humbled by your visit." Turning to address the younger captain standing discretely apart from the general, "Capitán Ramirez, I trust your journey from Española was uneventful?"

Pleased that he was recognized by the lady of the house, the young captain bowed and kissed her hand as well.

"Well worth the journey to be in your presence again, my lady," Capitán Ramirez respectfully answered.

María Isabella seemed pleased at her former lover's greeting, noticing his lips lingered not on her ring but on her hand itself.

"How may I help you gentlemen," she asked, as she motioned for them to sit on the couch; while she sat demurely on her chair.

The fire roared with warmth and light illuminating the elaborate tapestries that kept the drafts out of the manor.

"Doña María Isabella," spoke the general in a cautious tone. "I believe it is we, who will help you. Or more accurately, your husband and in turn, España herself."

He motioned for the soldiers standing outside the doorway to bring in the crate they had left in the foyer. María Isabella turned expectantly waiting to see with curiosity what they believed her husband may need.

The opened crate revealed the newest tools used as weapons for the military. Doña María Isabella stood up and walked over to the crate. Glee clearly on her face she picked up the newly acquired arquebus[88] and held it expertly, aiming it at the fireplace. Measuring one meter in length, the wooden and steel musket was heavy at four kilos. The men watched the Doña, quite surprised that she knew how to hold it with ease. Not many people knew that she and her husband bonded over their shared love of wine, ambition, and military weapons.

"How many are ready to be shipped?" she asked pointedly.

"Uh, well, ten crates with ten in them each. A hundred arquebus in total." General Marquez stammered his answer, having been shocked by the reactions of the Doña.

"Not enough," she thought out loud, "make it two hundred and have it sent to the ship I am boarding tomorrow morning. I will personally ensure that my husband and our valiant soldiers will have this to protect Spain's interests on the island." Smiling charmingly, she spoke to them as if she were discussing party favors for an event.

"Doña María Isabella… I do not think it is possible. That would leave our own infantry here with less than half of what they are expecting." The young captain's face registered disbelief that she would ask them for that number; his blue eyes scanned her face to see if she would be reasonable with her requests.

"It is very possible, Capitán Ramirez," she chided. "Here you can easily purchase more for our military. However, in the depths of hell where my esteemed husband has been sent, for the good of Spain, of course, he will not have ready access to these tools to protect Spain's interests against the

---

[88] Arquebus: a flintlock type of musket used to replace archers in the infantry. It would only shoot one .57 caliber bullet at a time before having to be reloaded using gunpowder and paper packing.

savages. Please… have it packed and moved before I board in the morning. I'm sure my cousin, Juan Ponce de Leon and my husband would ensure their gratitude is expressed in an appropriate and generous fashion."

Turning so she was in front of both men she inquired.

"I trust the slaves from Española that I ordered are on their way to my husband in Ponce already?"

Maldita mujer. General Marquez took a breath before he responded with assurance.

"Si, Doña María Isabella. They will be arriving approximately a week after you do. Your husband will be pleased at your gift to him."

Doña María Isabella finished the conversation and the visit by reminding them that they all must do their part for 'the glory of Spain.' Nodding to them both, she thanked them for their service and walked softly out of the room. The servants waited patiently, to escort them out of the home of Doña María Isabella. *Lord help the one who ever crosses her,* General Marquez thought to himself as he shook his head in disbelief.

The heavy shackles cut into his skin on his neck, wrists, and ankles. Olajuwon grimaced as he was led like cattle towards the plank of the ship. His blue-black skin glistened in the overbearing sun in Santo Domingo. The thickened scars, remnants of the first boat out of the Yoruba[89] territory, did nothing to dull the ache that permeated his flesh. Sweat dripped from his brow as he shuffled his bare feet onto the hot wood of the plank, the thin cotton shirt and pants clinging to his wide muscular frame did nothing to alleviate the heat, nor the squalid conditions he was about to experience... again.

Corralled below deck, eighty black men and twenty black women were compressed into a small room. With no room to sit they were forced to stand with the only ventilation coming in from the salty sea air of the deck, through the steel grate, located five feet above them. The suffocating heat coupled with the smell of urine and vomit made him nauseous, but he hid it. His demeanor showed no weakness; only strength. The ship creaked loudly as the anchor was lifted and sailed east. Olajuwon could tell by where the location of the sun overhead the direction they were sailing. Eight-foot high swells made it difficult for the one hundred captives to not topple over on one another.

Olajuwon entreated with his fervent prayers, *Olokun[90] guide us safely through the waters, so we may make land and soon, freedom!*

---

[89] Yoruba are an ethnic group of black Africans from the western and south-western region of Africa. Forcibly stolen, or sold into the Atlantic slave trade, they were considered to be property of the ones who purchased and traded them, and were ripped from their land, culture and families to work in subhuman conditions.

[90] Olokun is the Yoruba god who rules all bodies of water and has authority over other water deities